THE DREAM OF AMERICA.

"Like most others who have done the impossible, they were dreamers."

Peter Ebbesen, Danish immigrant 1868

MOESGAARD 1986

THE DREAM OF
A
★ AMERICA ★

CONTENTS

CONTENTS

THE DREAM OF A ★ AMERICA ★

INTRODUCTION.

Silent settlers

**"Some arrived in luxury
and some arrived in chain'
some were met with open arms
to some it was in vain
to some it looked like Paradise
to some it looked like Hell
the many, many millions
had different tales to tell;
but in their hearts they had a song
with hope as common theme
they had a goal, they had a will
but first of all a dream."**
                    Anonymous.

A new kind of awareness is growing in America; an ethnic and cultural awareness that in some ways ignores or even defies social, political and economic traditions. "Black is beautiful" or did "Indian Pride" are parallelled by many less profiled immigrant groups searching for their background or roots to define and preserve important elements of their identity. It is a different and complex awareness, carrying a lot of hope, because it seems to strenghten the understanding and tolerance of other people's rights to pursue and protect their dreams of America.

America was founded on the principles of liberty and equality at great human costs. That was the beginning of a long process, a strenuous and painful struggle to enable everybody to enjoy the same amount of freedom, a struggle which is still going on. It was started by the millions of individuals, groups and organizations who either chose or were forced to choose a life – different in so many ways – in the New World. Just as their interests, intentions and interactions differed, so did the background of these newcomers.

But in general they shared the visions of the promised land: America was a country where people had a chance to prosper, to get a piece of land they could call their own, honor their religion and political beliefs without oppression, pursue their own interpretations of happiness and individual development.

They came to a land where "success" was the keyword, where the winner was overwhelmingly rewarded – and the losers paid the price.

To the pioneers and the masses it was tough luck and labor, but at least they had a chance, at least they could work hard and keep the dream alive that they might make it, or that at least their children would.

America is a product of these many millions, and the process is still going on.

"Scandinavian immigrants left their homelands for economic rather than political or religious reasons. In America they found a political and social climate wholly compatible with their prior experience ... the seemingly limitless availability of farm land in America was an attractive prospect to landhungry people."

                    John F. Kennedy

Land *was* the major reason, if one reason should be singled out for Scandinavian emigration.

The Scandinavians did not seem like much in numbers, but it did not take them that long to establish a good reputation as honest hard working people. After all, compared to what they came from, the new country gave them a fair chance.

They established themselves in the Midwest, and many of them later moved further west. The Norwegians and the Swedes had a tendency to stick together more than the Danes, to build communities similar to those they left.

There are many examples of religious groups or whole villages leaving together and settling together. The Danes, however, tended to emigrate more as individuals and families. Perhaps Denmark's closer connections to Europe had prepared the Danes for a faster assimilation. Anyway: The Danes followed the same basic pattern as the other Scandinavians. They homesteaded or worked as farmhands, but they broke up faster, intermarried more often with other ethnic groups or "Americans" and took up the new language faster than the others. As a whole they assimilated faster than any other nationality.

Pictures from the exhibition: The Danish background

The departure

The crossing

This process of transition is the theme of this book. It is in itself a process, not a final product. It is part of a project of research that has produced several other books, films and exhibitions. The basis has been the exhibition created by The Danish National Museum and The Prehistoric Museum Moesgaard. It was shown in Copenhagen and Aarhus in 1984-85 with dozens of minor satellite exhibitions and events spread out all over Denmark.

Our first ambitions were to cover all the five Nordic countries but we soon learned that we would have to concentrate on our own country – Denmark. But in the process we also learned that by telling our story we were telling a "case" story that was valid also for the other Nordic countries. There were many similarities in the general European and national background, the experiences of crossing the Atlantic and facing a cultural shock were the same, and the settling patterns were almost identical – at least in the beginning.

Denmark did not experience extreme incidents of religious or political persecutions and deportations, though we had our share. And though we felt the crisis that hit Europe we never had a disaster like the Irish "potato famine" of the 1840s. We were scarred by war, but only the loss of Slesvig in Southern Denmark in 1864 was comparable to the bloodshed that soaked so many other countries.

We did not send so many of our " wretched and poor", they simply could not afford it. In Norway and Sweden many of these underprivileged were organized or organized themselves into emigration groups. On the whole, Denmark probably sent more "middle class" members than any other country.

We may very well be one of the national or ethnic groups best used as an example of the *general* or *average* pattern of emigration.

This general pattern is expressed in the exhibition as well as in this book even though it primarily uses Danish examples. The progression covers the social, political, economical and cultural *background,* the *push-and-pull* factors, the *crossing* of the Atlantic, the *arrival* in the New World, the *settling,* and the *assimilation.*

Finally, I would very much like to express my gratitude and acknowledgement to all the people who have worked hard to make this project possible, and I sincerely hope that others will continue what we have started.

Stig Thornsohn

Life in the city –

and on the prairie

THE MOESGAARD EXHIBITION 1985

WHY DID THEY LEAVE?

About 52 million Europeans emigrated to overseas countries between 1840 and 1914, thus helping to shape the modern world. About 35 million came to America, a migration of young, strong people who helped make that country flourish into a world power.

300,000 of the emigrants came from Denmark and formed a vital minority which still prospers there. What prompted these Danish men and women to emigrate?

Denmark a Piece in the Big Pattern

The Danish overseas emigration has its own exciting history based on certain conditions in Denmark. Yet Denmark comprised only a minute part of the total European picture. It was a phenomenon which cut across all frontiers, an almost imperceptible mass movement which began out along the west coast of Europe where they knew the sea and about the lands far beyond. Gradually it spread like fever throughout the continent among the young people when they heard about the marvelous riches and the great opportunities in the New World.

Emigration began in England. As the British Empire grew, poor farmers and laborers went out to the new colonies. Around 1800 the British government realized the advantages of emigration: it was able to solve the serious problem of unemployment and at the same time consolidated British colonialism by settling British subjects abroad. Their travel expenses were paid and frequently in addition they received money to establish themselves. A considerable number of convicts from British prisons were also relocated abroad.

The next great wave of immigrants to the U.S. came from Ireland. In 1846 the potato crop failed and famine followed. Over the next 20 years (1846-66) more than half the Irish population emigrated to America. The Irish cut a wide swath through all levels of American society.

In Norway emigration also started early. In this nation of many sailors, the poor farmers around the fiords learned about America. In 1825 the first emigrant vessel left Bergen bound for America. After Ireland, Norway had the greatest percentage of emigrants.

Beginning in the 1850s the German emigrants came up the Rhine and Elbe Rivers in droves and left from Hamburg, Bremen, and Antwerp for America.

In the 1860s emigration fever reached Denmark. The dream about America had been vivid in people's minds as early as in the 1830s when Christian Winther wrote his famous poem, "The Flight to America", and Hans Christian Andersen wrote a song with the following refrain: "A pity that America should be so far away."

An unknown number of Danish adventurers left after 1848 for California, lured by rumors of great gold strikes, and in the following years the thought of "streets paved with gold" tempted an increasing number to emigrate. In the 1860s the number exceeded 1,000 Danes a year.

The Size of the Danish Emigration

No exact number of Danish emigrants before 1868 is known. A bill was passed that year stating that the agents had to register their customers with the police to ensure that the contracts concerning transportation were fulfilled. The police registers and the American immigration files provide us with the following figures.

Danish Immigrants

1820-67 (estimated)	14,000
1868-1914	287,000
1915-32	80,500
Total (1820-1932)	381,500

In the period up to World War II it is estimated that something like 400,000 Danes got a one-way ticket and settled overseas. How many of them returned home is not known unfortunately, but the number before 1900 is presumably very low.

During the great emigration boom before World War I some 6,000 people emigrated each year. As a comparison the corresponding figure in the 1970s was 4,000 per year, but the population in Denmark was close to 5,000,000. The annual 6,000 emigrants before 1914 came out of a population of less than 3,000,000. This means that about one out of every ten Danes emigrated overseas. One out of every six Norwegians emigrated to America. This kind af loss in population seriously affected those who remained behind.

By far the greatest number of emigrants were young people between 15 and 25, and through several decades the most efficient man-power was greatly diminished. In Denmark more men than women emigrated, thus upsetting the natural balance between the sexes. Not until the period before World War II was the balance restored.

Which Part of Denmark Did They Come From?

The idea of emigrating spread from farm to farm, from county to county. Still the emigrating Danes did not fall into a uniform pattern. In some areas the "fever" hit early and an emigration tradition was developed over decades. In other areas the idea never dawned or it held little appeal.

On one of the big emigrant vessels leaving Copenhagen before 1900 with 1,000 Danes, a typical distribution would be as follows: 192 from Copenhagen, 398 from the rest of Sjælland, Lolland and Falster, while 410 of the passengers would come from Jutland. By comparing these emigrant-figures to the population of their home counties, a clear picture emerges of where the "emigration fever" took hold and where it failed. In Lolland-Falster and Bornholm almost 14 out of every 100 emigrated. In central Jutland only three per 100 left. Similarly low figures are found for North Sjælland where Copenhagen, not America, was the attracting magnet. As far as central Jutland is concerned the reason is probably that the large-scale emigration took place at the same time as the cultivation of the heath, and

everybody could acquire land for farming. This was Denmark's own prairie and land was plentiful, thus the low figures of emigration. Above all emigration expressed unrest among the young people. Departure from the home county was the youth rebellion of that time. The number of young people migrating within Denmark greatly exceeded the number of emigrants. The young people in the rural areas were disenchanted. They could not count on inheriting land, but faced the prospect of working as farm-hands. They saw their best hopes as laborers in the growing industries of the cities. After the introduction of obligatory education, young people were far better informed about the world around them. The modern railways rapidly took them to the gay life in the city. They would have preferred to stay in the country as independent farmers, but the wages for farmhands and maids amounted to approximately 100 Danish crowns per year; they would never be able to save up enough money to buy their own land.

This can clearly be seen in the geographic distribution of the emigration. Areas with high prices for land and dominated by large estate owners, as in Lolland-Falster, Langeland and southern Funen had a high rate of emigration. Not only did poor economic prospects offer problems, but love did so as well. A young couple might make love in their master's barn, but they could never afford to marry until they had some land of their own to work. So off they went by train to the nearest town to get a job, and frequently they went to the emigration agencies in Copenhagen and headed off for the States.

If we examine the ratio of farmers to city-dwellers, the majority of Danish emigrants came from the capital city and from the towns, which was not the case in Norway or Sweden. Many of these townsmen, however, had tried in vain to make a living in the city and then made the great decision to go to the American prairie.

Young women often went to the nearest town, got a job there – they formed a cheaper labor force than did the men – whereas young men went directly to America to homestead on the prairie. Often young lovers seeking an economic base for a marriage left together. Conditions around 1850 accounted for an average marrying age of 32 years for men and 29 for women. They could not count on setting up their own households before then.

The number of emigrants from each county 1868-1900.

Emigration Rose When the Grain Prices Fell

Until this era the Danish economy and trade had been dominated by agriculture, but now an exodus of people was seen from Danish farming. This was caused by a great many things; among these was an immense increase in rural population since 1800. More children survived infancy, the average age rose and the rate of mortality fell due to better nutrition and improved medical care. Every farm reared 10 to 12 children, and only one or perhaps two might take over the farm. The rest faced a future as farmhands or maids. Another reason for the exodus was a decline in the price of grain. The first immigrants in America cultivated the prairie, and their excess crop of corn and wheat was exported to Europe, thus dropping prices dangerously on the European market, often to such an extent that the European farms simply did not pay off. This accounted for the vast emigration from Sweden and Norway towards the end of the 1860s.

Denmark was also hit by the crisis, but was better equipped to face it. Agriculture was changed from grain to animal products. The hogs and the chickens were fed corn and grain, and huge areas were laid out for grassland and turnip

fields. Animal farming demanded more labor; milkmaids and farm-hands were in demand. Their wages did improve, and small plots of land were developed to keep the labor force in the country. This change within agriculture explains why Danish emigration never reached the same high levels as in Norway and Sweden. In the other Scandinavian countries industry was less developed than in Denmark and the Danish towns were far better equipped to absorb the migration from the rural areas which began around the 1850s. The railway towns – a typically Danish phenomenon – employed some and many others found jobs in Copenhagen, although unemployment there often reached 40 to 50 % during the winter months.

Craftsmen were another group squeezed out during the industrialization. Their products were now being mass-produced by machines. They then faced a choice between working as unskilled laborers in the factories or emigration. Traditionally they travelled in Europe, originally as part of their education. Then it became a desperate attempt to find employment, and America offered new opportunities. The blacksmiths faced the most severe problems. Out of 100 blacksmiths from Danish towns, no less than 56 emigrated before 1900, many of them taking along families.

The road mender. Some were too poor to try their luck.

Export of Paupers and Criminals

Many Danish communities solved their social problems silently and discreetly by sending their paupers to America on a one-way ticket. This was far cheaper than relief money for years. In 1880 one of the major immigration agents seized the opportunity to make a fortune and thus sent the following letter to all Danish parish councils.

As this practice was generally condemned by the Ministry of Justice we have no information as to how many customers the immigration agent won through this letter. The Copenhagen Police Director also took advantage of the opportunity to rid himself of offensive criminals as well as troublesome politicians like the two Socialist-leaders, Pio and Geleff. But when the American Press disclosed that a Danish coiner had been exported, Copenhagen at least stopped this practice.

J. Rath   *Copenhagen, February 1880*
Steamship Co.
Nyhavn 13
Copenhagen C.

To the honorable chairman of the parish council.

The undersigned representative of the Steamship Co. "Allan Line", whose ships convey passengers to America, takes the liberty of sending You some folders for Your inspection, and I offer my assistance concerning the transportation of such people who are a constant burden to the community. Ensuring a fair and exact treatment to gain Your confidence, I beg to inform You that over a considerable period I have been responsible for the dispatch of persons expelled by the Copenhagen Police and Poor-law authorities in Copenhagen and in other towns.

Should similar cases arise, I beg You to bear my above services in mind.

Yours very respectfully,
J. Rath

The Flight from Slesvig after 1864

The loss of Slesvig-Holstein in 1864 was universally mourned. The grief was deepest in the pro-Danish part between Kolding and the present border, which now came under Prussian rule. Many of the young people in North Slesvig refused to be ruled by Germany. They could not come to terms with the use of German language in their schools and their churches, but most of all they objected to several years of military service in the Prussian army. Some opted to Denmark, but the German rule gave rise to a veritable exodus from North-Slesvig to America. Population statistics show that before 1905 some 54,000 Slesvigers left the county, which only had about 150,000 inhabitants. In the U.S. they probably settled where other Danes had settled before them. When, according to U.S.'s statistics, so many Danes married German immigrants, it is most likely that they came from North Slesvig instead. They were German citizens although they spoke and felt like other Danes.

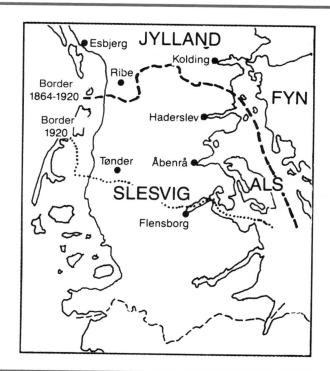

16

To America for God's Sake

The majority left for economic reasons, but a small group were drawn to the States for religious reasons. They were mainly Mormons who were converted by missionaries sent to Denmark in 1849. These missionaries came from Salt Lake City, Utah, and promised that heaven could be found there. All their adherents were to go there – to this "Zion" – and the missionaries made an amazing number of converts in Denmark. More than 16,000 Danes emigrated to Utah which still to this day is strongly marked by Danes. Many shop signs carry names such as Sorensen and Pedersen. The Mormon converts chiefly came from northern Jutland (51 %) and Copenhagen (37 %), and were almost always from among the poor. The Mormon Church covered the travel expenses, but the money had to be paid back when the immigrants had settled down in Utah. These Mormons went on specially chartered boats. Many ships departed, often from Aalborg, and with a full-bearded missionary leading the passengers in song. These emigrant vessels differed from other boats because the women far outnumbered the men. Women were more susceptible to religious movements outside the established church.

America, the Great Attraction

This article thus far discusses economic, social, religious and political reasons which prompted Danes to emigrate. These people were also tempted and pulled towards the States through promises of gold and property. These promises spread through propaganda pamphlets which

„Everything is bigger over here!"

reached even the most out-of-the-way places. For the average Dane, the major attraction in America was not so much a life as a gold prospector, rather was it the possibility of settling down on a farm of his own. In 1862 Congress passed a bill stating that irrespective of nationality anyone could get a piece of land on the prairie, a homestead of 160 acres. This was every farm-hand's dream. The Homestead Act was the main reason why 89 % of all emigrating Danes chose America. The journey to the prairie, which used to take months, was made easy when the railroads were built in the 1860s. The railroad companies needed passengers, so they sent their agents to Europe with thousands of advertizing bills which were distributed in every country.

The big transatlantic shipping companies also made a profit off the emigrants. They placed agents in all embarkation harbors and in many widely-scattered towns. These agents tried to persuade people to emigrate. The idea of "seeking your fortune" in America could be seen on every lamppost and billboard. The first emigrants wrote letters home telling about the high wages and the rich prairie land. The railroad companies handed out paper and stamps to the farmers so that they could write home and attract some new passengers. This huge American publicity drive spread into Denmark through the agents of the shipping companies. From the 1870s the railroad and shipping companies went so far as to provide free crossings to Europe for thousands of well-established farmers, provided they then came up with new passengers for the ships and railroads.

These "Yankees" then returned to their home counties and by their well-to-do attire and "ten-gallon hats" they symbolized the prosperity over there. They received 15 Danish crowns, a small fortune in those days, for every new emigrant they brought back to the States, and many of them managed to lure huge groups into leaving with them. The Americans had a great economic interest in increasing emigration. Strong, energetic young people were exposed to a heavy "pull" from the States, just as the miserable Danish social conditions "pushed" many people out of the country.

This "push and pull" effect has been debated frequently over the last decades. The same effects work today on millions of people from Turkey, Pakistan, Yugoslavia and many other countries that send people in droves into Europe. The emigrants of today experience a similar push: unemployment and poverty in the home country; and a pull: jobs, the dream of high wages and a social security system like the one in Denmark.

Which is stronger: the tempting ovations from the rich, faraway land, or the miserable conditions in their home country?

In the 1930's, "shrewd" scholars thought that the rises and declines in the number of emigrants matched the periods of growth and recession in the U.S. more than in Europe. Their conclusion was that the American pull was stronger than the European push. This theory looks very plausible once it is plotted out in diagrams, but the relationship is far more complex. It concerned thousands of Danish and millions of European people, each of them having his own individual and very personal destiny and reasons for emigrating. A few were the "black sheep" of the family, sent away "for free"; others left because of unhappy love or because they were having a baby out of wedlock. This exodus cannot possibly be attributed to mere economic reasons, let alone to information concerning the American trade outlook. Emigrant letters and memoirs also reveal that apart from careful deliberation, strong emotions prevailed when the great decision about emigration was made.

Nevertheless statistics show that the dream of better conditions in life played an important role in their considerations. The majority of the Danish emigrants settled down on the prairie in Nebraska and Iowa as farmers. For many the new life was very harsh. To wrest the first crop from the prairie took blood, sweat and tears over many years. On top of this came longings for the homeland and relatives. Many people have often pondered the question. Was emigrating from Denmark the right step to take?

To many the answer has been affirmative, at least for their children. In the Danish-American churches a hymn expressed it in this way:

"that others may reap what we have secured,
and happily live where we have endured."

Letters from „over there" described the daily toil, but also the great opportunities. They nourished dreams and induced many to make „the big decision". Oil painting from 1835.

THE DENMARK THEY LEFT.

Tradition and Transition in an Agrarian Society

During the revolutionary decade in America, 1770-80, several decisive changes occurred in Danish society. Since the middle ages Danish Agriculture had been characterized by large estate owners and the common field system: the majority of the land was owned by the aristocracy and farmed by copyholders who paid fees such as manorial dues, frequently as tithes paid in kind or villeinage. These villeins, or small farmers, lived in communal villages consisting of a cluster of farmhouses and common fields which were cultivated collectively. Since each farmer's land was scattered all over the common field, everyone had both good and poor land to work. This system was changed radically in the 1780s due to the rise in industry, particularly in England, which created a strong demand for foodstuffs in the urban economic centers. Denmark began to export grain to help meet this demand.

Changing Modes of Production – and a Changing Landscape

The old mode of production then proved unprofitable; no export could be based on the output of manorial farms. Capital was needed as well as a change in property ownership. This was accomplished by enabling the copyholders to buy their own farms. Thus their personal legal dependency on the aristocracy disappeared, though it was replaced by another dependency: economic. For the landed gentry the purpose of the reforms was to channel capital into their own farms.

This capital was necessary to render their estates more efficient and to increase production for the lucrative export market. Another important result of the reform was that the Danish scenery was radically altered. The farms had come to include the adjoining lands which prompted many farmers to move away from the village and onto their own land. The modern-day Danish landscape with its numerous individual farmhouses standing on their own ground was established in this way.

These reforms also called for a restructuring within the agricultural sector. Not all copyholders were able to buy their farms, so new class distinctions arose in the country: in addition to the division between the aristocracy and the copyholders, a new distinction was made between the freeholders and the landless farmers. The latter group was definitely the largest and their conditions deteriorated severely. Earlier they had benefitted to a certain extent from the common rights of the communal village.

Progress and Poverty

After a serious crisis in the first decades of the 19th century, Danish agriculture began to experience economic growth, especially after 1840. The export of grain to England was still the motivating factor. More and more copyholders became freeholders, but because of the considerable growth in population, the number of landless farmers also increased dramatically.

Around 1870, American grain began to replace the Danish exports to England. Danish farmers then changed their production to animal products such as butter and bacon. At the same time the farmers united in cooperative undertakings to be able to compete with the financially strong estates of the landed aristocracy.

„Traditional" village: the farms still cluster around the church.

„Modern" landscape: outlying farmhouses standing on their own ground.

Numerous cooperative dairies and slaughterhouses were established in the 1880s and 90s. Thus the majority of farmers survived the crisis, but for the majority of farm laborers this offered little improvement. Small farmers and farm laborers had to watch silently as other groups in Danish society made considerable advances.

Small Farmers and Servants

The role of the small farmers was established by the beginning of the 19th century: he was to help the freeholders run their farms and constituted the labor force necessary to run the farms and the large estates. His own land was not enough to support him and his family.

The son of a small farmer writes the following about his home around 1890:

"The small eight-acre farm of poor, sandy topsoil on the northeast side of Hammer Hills in Vendsyssel could neither feed nor clothe a family, so my father had to work as a day-laborer, usually on big farms far from home ... He worked on these farms for several years. His main problem was that the farm had to be as close as possible to home because he never had a bicycle. Periodically his work was so far away from home that he only came home late Saturday night. He left again on Monday morning at around four to arrive in time for work ... During busy periods such as the spring planting and fall harvest, my mother often joined him at work, for as long as she had the strength to do so ..."
(*Tales from a Vendelbo Boy*, Niels Anesen.)

20

The great need for farm land meant that areas which until then had been unused were tilled, and in some areas, estates and farms were developed in order to procure more cottages and small plots for the farm laborers. None of these plots, however, was able to sustain a family. The demand for land caused prices to go up, and the income of a small farmer was not enough for him to ever buy more land. Many sons of freeholders experienced the disastrous effect of this situation: when the oldest son took over the farm after his father, the other sons often were forced to a lower rung on the social ladder, becoming hired hands or leaving for the cities.

The Daily Bread

The entire family of a farmhand helped tend what little land they had and the livestock, too, if they had a cow or a couple of pigs. The majority, however, had to earn their daily bread by working as farmhands wherever they could. Farmhands were generally hired for one or two days, when the farmers needed them, either for plowing, harrowing, tending to cattle, harvesting or threshing. When the work was done, they could return home. Very few had so much work that they could manage without any problems throughout the year.

Unemployment was high among farmhands, particularly in winter. When the threshing was done, they had to begin again, this time cutting wood, plowing snow or clearing beds for the railways. In early spring there was scarcely any work, and the meager provisions were almost used up. Hunger had begun to gnaw and the next harvest was a long way off. The woman toiled at home, raised vegetables, kept chickens and perhaps a couple of sheep so that she could make most of the clothes for the family. Often she had a large family of at least six or seven children, and the many pregnancies and deliveries sapped her strength.

"Hard years and many childbirths had ruined her strong figure, her health, her high spirits, and she had lost most of her thick hair. She wandered around in an endless mess with one child on her arm near her flat bosom, one on her apron strings and one under her heart, as the saying goes. The ideal of a clean home had long been abandoned. If only she could save it from being too dirty. The children, born with pain and often disease as well, and for whom he (the father) toiled in unending worry, were actually the only single tie they had to each other and to life."
(From a Danish story, 1894. "Der er et yndigt land" by Edvard Egebjerg)

Like her husband, the small farmer's wife only found work intermittently. She might be used during the harvest or she turned up when it was wash day or slaughtering time. When dairying gradually got started in the 1880s, many farmers' wives found employment as milkmaids. They arrived at five in the morning and then again late in the afternoon. Day laborers were paid in various ways. While working on the farm they were fed, and as payment they were allotted a certain amount of grain, potatoes or firewood to take home. Since this rarely covered the need of the family, they frequently filled their pockets with pig swill before they went home in the evening. The pay might also include grazing privileges in the farm's fields, or permission to use draft animals when they had to plow their own fields. Usually money was the smallest part of the pay.

When famine seemed imminent, the fields were dug again and again in the hope of finding even the very last potatoes. Periods of actual famine, like those in Ireland and Sweden, were not seen in Denmark. They coped, although they sometimes were on the verge of starvation. The children took part in the work. They helped in the household and tended cattle. It was not uncommon, however, for a small farmer to send his children away at the age of seven or eight to serve on other farms; he simply could not afford to keep them at home. He then settled the issue of pay for the child with the farmer. It usually consisted of food and lodging, a pair of wooden clogs and a pair of trousers per year. A boy might start tending the cattle or sheep, fetching firewood or helping in the stables. A girl started as a goose-girl and worked with the other women in the household. Their duties increased as they grew older. Education was haphazard and casual, despite the fact that it was compulsory for seven years.

As time went by the children became part of the huge group of servants who worked under miserable conditions on the country's many estates.

Reapers in the fields of an estate in Lolland, ab. 1880. These people were hired for the harvest season only.

The ploughman embodied the Danish peasantry – immortalized on the old five hundred kroner note.

The Plight of the Farmhands

During the 1850s there were around 150,000 farmhands in service. The meager wages offered no possibility for ever buying one's own land. On top of this the work was hard and the laborers were subject to domestic discipline. The master had a right to punish his servants if he thought it necessary. This discipline applied to girls until they were 16 and for boys until the age of 18. How often the master actually did discipline his laborers depended entirely on his temperament. Combined with very poor material conditions, a hot-tempered master could make life intolerable for the farmhands. From a political point of view servants might also have been considered oppressed. In 1849 the Danish Constitution introduced what was called general franchise. This did not include women or servants, however, since they could not meet the constitutional requirement of owning property.

The Danish author, Jeppe Aakjær, was one of the first people who sought to improve conditions for the farmhands by writing articles in newspapers and magazines, and by informing people at meetings about their plight.

In an article from *Skive Folkeblad,* March 14, 1890, he wrote the following:

"... Through a door which was ajar I glimpsed a pale, freckled face, that of the sick man. I edged into the room through the narrow opening, and was now in a room which I took to be the farmhand's room. What a place to put this man! Here the animals stood in their foul and messy stalls. His room occupied a corner of the barn, not much cozier than the other stalls. It was separated from the rest by two clay walls which had been kicked down in several places by the horses. Part of the wall was also missing above the door made of dirty, old planks. As the door could not

After 30 years of hard work as farmhand and maid this couple built their own house in 1908. In 1899 the Danish State initiated a legislation to promote the parcelling out of large farms into smallholdings. The plots were not big enough to sustain a family (1-10 acres), so the bigger farms and the estates could still get workers when they needed them.

be closed, it let the stench from the barn flow unhindered over the sick man ...

What little light reached the chamber sneaked in through half a window where one pane was broken and the hole plugged with a pair of old trousers. A wobbly cupboard, leaning against the wall and holding a couple of dirty shirts, took up most of the space not occupied by the wooden bed, so it was not possible for two people to pass each other. Such was the room where this young man lay, the thin covers showing his skinny legs and arms. On all sides he was surrounded by moldy, reeking bedstraw. For six weeks he had been left here in this abominable filth ...

And the maid's room, if she had one, was not much better, even though she often lived under the same roof as her master and mistress. Her room was usually found under the stairs or in a remote corner of the house. Always with as little elbow-room as possible. Frequently her room also functioned as a storeroom for wool, tools and implements of all sorts ..."

Industrialization – New Possibilities?

The hope of work in the growing industries first led the farmhands to the towns, and in the latter half of the 19th century about 300,000 people migrated from rural to urban areas. This did not automatically improve their lot. Unemployment in some areas reached 50 %. Housing conditions were miserable due to speculation in buildings put up cheaply and quickly for the many new arrivals. Construction was booming. On the open land outside the old part of Copenhagen one tenement after another shot up. This offered temporary jobs for some, but for the occupants it only meant that their tiny farmhouse had been exchanged for a cramped one-bedroom apartment which was gradually hemmed in by more tenements.

Until the 1870s Danish industry had developed modestly and sporadically. Minor industries and workshops grew in the provincial towns, and only Copenhagen had one or two of the larger factories. Not until the 1890s did the real industrialization begin. After the turn of the century industrial growth was extensive enough to absorb the labor force.

The Old Town: The Past Alive

The river divides the town in two, the pharmacy (1571) can be seen in the back.

During the first half of the 19th century – at the time of Hans Christian Andersen – the majority of the Danish population lived in the country as farmers. With Copenhagen, capitol and residential city, as the only exception, Danish towns were small, between 1000 and 4000 inhabitants.

Distanced some 20 miles from each other, the towns were scattered all over the country. Despite their smallness, they played an important role in the financial situation of the kingdom. Certain trades could only be performed in the towns, just as all import and export had to take place through these towns. The explanation is close at hand: at the town gate or at the town harbour, a duty was put on the goods. This duty – the so-called excise – went into the coffers of the state, the sales tax of those days.

The bill of freedom of trade from 1857, the development of roads and railroads as well as the beginning industrialization meant radical changes of the medieval patterns of habitation. A close network of new railway towns arose and the old market towns grew. One of the towns with a very rapid development was Århus, which grew from a medium-sized market town to the second largest city in Denmark.

A young man, Peter Holm, realized that this development entailed a disapperance of the old town culture; this particularly concerned minor trades which slowly but surely gave way to industrialization. Around 1900 open-air museums were not unknown, but Peter Holm got the bright idea to preserve market town culture for posterity. At a great exhibition in Århus in 1909 Peter Holm could show his first house: an old merchant's house from 1597. Cartoonists ridiculed his interest in this ancient rubbish, but nevertheless he succeeded in getting the house re-erected in the city gardens, the present botanical gardens.

Gradually he bought more and more houses, not only from Århus, but from market towns all over Denmark. Today his museum, The Old Town, comprises more than 60 houses, dating from the 16th century up to the 19th century. When strolling down the narrow cobbled lanes, one feels carried back to a drowzy little market town, expecting every moment to bump into figures from Hans Christian Andersen's fairy tales.

Det gjøres herved vitterligt at

fra Dags Dato er at ansee for Borger i „Den gamle By"

Borgmestergaarden den

The maintenance of the old buildings is very expensive. The houses suffer under today's pollution. Consequently the museum has started a financial backing society, called Citizens of The Old Town, and all members receive a document confirming their citizenship, issued by the mayor of The Old Town.

Some of the buildings hold workshops and small stores. In the oldest house in the town from 1571 a distinguished pharmacy is established. Here the pharmacist's magic powers are emphasized through strange creatures like crocodiles and dogfish, or sheer phantoms like a "sea-monkey". There are also workshops for vanishing trades like hatters, fringe-makers, needle-makers and soaperies. "An army marches on its stomach" – and the museum also holds a brewery and a distillery. Various special collections can be seen at the museum, e.g. collections of China, furniture, stoves, musical instruments, textiles and toys. The Old Town is thus in many ways a unique museum of North European town culture.

Old-fashioned market and festive parades during the Århus festival week.

SCANDINAVIAN-AMERICAN LINE

CONVENIENT ROUTE
TO AND FROM
ALL PARTS OF EUROPE

CROSSING THE ATLANTIC.

Departure from Larsens Plads, Copenhagen. Painting by Edvard Petersen, 1890.

THINGVALLA-LINIEN.

Kahytspriser 1897.

BILLETTER

fra

Kjøbenhavn, Malmø, Helsingborg, Frederikshavn, Gøteborg, Christiania og **Christianssand**

til

NEW YORK

udstedes til følgende Priser for Afrejse

efter „Thingvalla"s Afgang

(den 16. Marts):

1ste Kahyt.

Med Dampskibene „Amerika" og „Hekla"	Kr. 225
Med Dampskibene „Thingvalla", „Island" og „Norge"	- 215

NB. I „Amerika": Køjeplads i Kamrene A, B og C samt i 2 Køjers Kamre koster **Kr. 50** extra pr. enkelt Tur.
I „Hekla": Køjeplads i Kamrene A og B koster **Kr. 25** extra pr. enkelt Tur.

Tur- og Returbilletter, gyldige til alle Skibene	- 420

2den Kahyt.

Med alle Skibene	Kr. 180
s/s „Island"s indvendige Kamre E & F (Familier med Børn maa ikke indskrives)	- 170
Tur- og Returbilletter, gyldige til alle Skibene	- 342

Boarding and farewell on an emigrant ship in 1871. For most emigrants there was no way back. The severing of ties with family and friends was permanent.

Right: The crossing by sailing ships might last more than 2 months. The list of provisions shows that the passengers themselves were required to take along kitchen utensils and provisions for 10 weeks. A grown person needed a supply of 70 pounds of bread, 8 pounds of butter, 24 pounds of meat, 10 pounds of pork, 1 keg of herring, 3/8 barrel of potatoes, 20 pounds of rye or barley flour, 1/2 skjeppe (ca. 1/4 bushel) peas, 1/2 skjeppe pearled barley, 3 pounds of coffee, 3 pounds of sugar, 2 1/2 pounds of syrup, and a little salt, pepper, vinegar, and onions. The skipper provided 3 potter, about 3 quarts, of water for each passenger per day.

On April 1st we bade them all goodbye, and Father took us to Copenhagen to see us aboard. It was the last time I saw my father.

The trip across the Atlantic was very hard, as we had to take steerage, because that was the cheapest, and the ship was very crowded. We had only one bunk for the five of us. My baby, little Dagmar, who was then ten months old, was cross the whole trip. She was used to nurse my breasts, but being seasick I had no milk. The other two, Mary and Niels, were as good as gold, but it was hard, for we could not undress on the whole trip. We did not have a cabin for ourselves, but were in a large room, big enough for one hundred to one hundred sixty, or maybe more, which was all filled with two tier bunks – one above the other.

Most of the passengers in that room were Polish or southern Germans, with a very few Scandinavians, but little we cared who they were, just so we were left alone. That was nearly impossible for if the party in

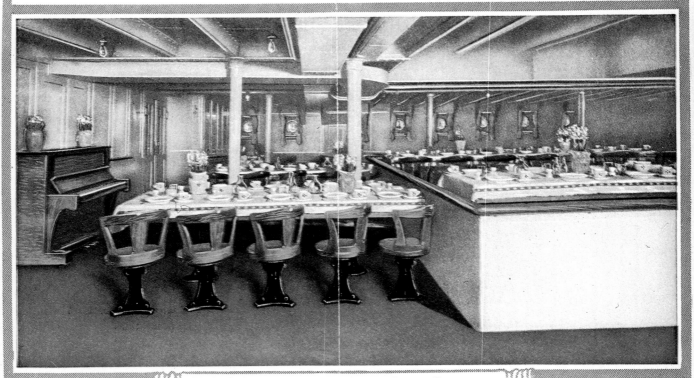

Scandinavian-American Line

Third Class

A CORNER OF A THIRD CLASS DINING ROOM

the bunk above us felt nauseated, as most of them did, he just vomited right past the bed underneath and down on the floor. There it stayed until twice a day some sailor came and tried to sweep it up with a coarse broom made of birch branches. Most of these people would sit and pick vermin out of their clothes and throw them on the floor.

When it came to mealtime, everyone lined up in a long row, and each brought his plate to the place where the big soup kettle was. We had two tin plates such as the steamship agent told us to buy, and Peter brought for the five of us in them. Even if we were sick, we had to try to eat. They always served soup of some kind, but it all seemed to be cooked in the same kettle, for it seemed tasteless and uneatable.

But all things came to an end and so did that voyage!

From: *The Life History of Mrs. Bertha Josephsen Anderson.*
      The Bridge 1983.

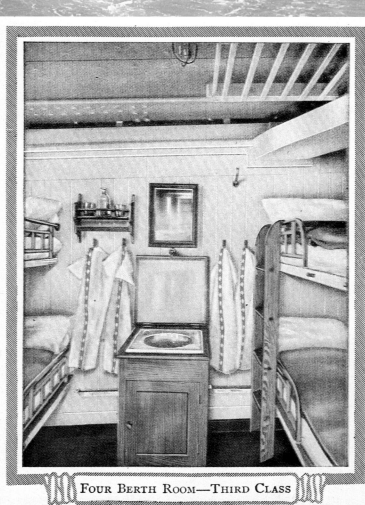

FOUR BERTH ROOM—THIRD CLASS

„Frederik 8." was the first steamship in the world accomodating emigrants on 3rd class in two, four, or six berth rooms.
Color pictures from a brochure produced in America ab. 1920 by the DFDS.

The Crossing

In 1868 the Danish government, as the first in the world, passed a special bill concerning emigrants. This was meant as a regulation of the market and also to ensure that the company agents did not take advantage of the emigrants. The bill was for the protection of the emigrants as it called upon the company to pay the return fare, in case the emigrant was refused admission at Ellis Island. A contract was signed between the company and the emigrant, and copies of these were sent to the police authorities in Copenhagen. This explains why we have much more thorough information of emigrants and their backgrounds than other European countries.

The police were to supervise provisions, water, life-saving equipment and cargo. All emigrants had to have a medical check-up and the crew should also include a doctor. All these precautions meant that only a few Danes were turned away at the immigration control on Ellis Island.

During the 1860s and 70s steamers replaced sails on the transatlantic routes. This meant briefer crossings and scheduled departures and arrivals. 7-8 weeks under sails were now reduced to about 2 weeks on a steamer from Copenhagen to New York.

Until 1880 Danish emigrants went by German and English companies, in particular Hapag, Norddeutscher Lloyd, Cunard, Inman and Allan Lines, but in 1880 the Danish Thingvalla Line was established. During the 18 years of its existence the Thingvalla Line carried some 155.000 Scandinavians, mostly Norwegians and Swedes, to America from Copenhagen via Gothenburg and Christiania (Oslo) to New York. A series of shipwrecks befell the company, however, and in 1898 the great company DFDS took over. "The Scandinavia-America Line" was established and ran until 1936.

On the Thingvalla Line emigrants travelled either as cabin passengers or as steerage passengers. 11 out of 12 passengers went on steerage. In the 1880s a steerage fare cost around 100 dkr, corresponding almost to the annual income of a farmhand. Growing competition cut the prices somewhat in the 1890s, but still it was beyond most farmhand families, as they were paid in kind mainly. Thus the system of prepaid tickets: the head of the family emigrated and worked until he had made enough money to send tickets for the rest of the family. Around one third of all emigrants travelled on these prepaid tickets.

Scenes from the Atlantic crossing. Photographed by the ship's doctor, A. Gramstrup.

A Shipwreck.
The overseas passages often met with disasters, rapidly affecting the companies involved, because the number of passengers fell drastically. During its 16 years, the Thingvalla Line lost three ships. A serious disaster occurred in 1888 on the Atlantic Ocean with the collision of two of the company's ships. The sea was calm, but due to heavy fog and rain, the Thingvalla rammed the starboard side of the Geiser, bound for Copenhagen. Panic set in on the Geiser and after 5 minutes the ship broke in two and sank. Out of 140 only 14 passengers and 17 members of the crew were rescued on board the Thingvalla. Later in the day all passengers were carried into safety on another boat as the bow of the Thingvalla was severely damaged. By using an American fishing boat as a kind of emergency rudder, the captain succeeded in sailing the ship backwards to Halifax. What caused this notorious shipwreck has never been clarified, but the consequences were that east- and west-bound sea lanes were now separated by more than 50 miles.

The Goshawk
The inquiry offered no solution to the tragic incident. There was no reasonable explanation to why the two ships collided and why the Geiser went down. Thomas Dinesen, Karen Blixen's father, who emigrated on the Geiser before it went down, tells us that off Newfoundland a goshawk settled in the rigging of the main mast. One of the passengers insisted on shooting it, but the sailors chased it away. Some time later it returned and settled wearily in the rigging. Again they made it fly away but ,,at that moment a shot rang out. The bird threw itself up in the air and sailed out over the sea on widespread wings. This brings bad luck, the sailors said. The bird returned after an hour and settled in the topsail. The light feathers above its claws were bloody. It sat for a little while, ditheringly, then fell down onto the deck, dead. On August 14, 1888 the Geiser was lost on this position." Boganis' Hunting Letters.

ISLAND OF TEARS

Ellis Island –
a small island of about 24 acres in New York harbour,
was the first encounter with the New World for many immigrants.
In an effort to control immigration
it served as the eye of the needle,
through which all newcomers had to pass.

By far the greatest number of immigrants arrived at New York. Of the 5.5 million who arrived in America between 1820 and 1860, some 3.7 million debarked there. 550,000 arrived in New Orleans, while 380,000 went to Boston, and both Philadelphia and Baltimore each received 250,000. By 1890 more than 4/5 of the new arrivals came to New York, and by the turn of the century almost all new immigrants passed the Statue of Liberty, whose torch of freedom was held high as a welcome to the incoming masses. Until 1855 when an old fort, Castle Garden (formerly a circus), was made into a receiving station, immigration control had been very lax. The reception was a formality and the American authorities were mainly concerned with hurrying the immigrants on toward their final destinations.

At Castle Garden, which served as an immigrant reception center from 1855 to 1892, strict regulations were set up for processing as many as 4,000 immigrants a day during the peak season. The mentally ill, crippled and blind people, those with infectious diseases and the very poor – all those deemed to be a strain on society – were turned away. The railroads and shipping companies had their agents there, and an efficient labor exchange was established. The entire operation was financed by an immigration tax of $ 1.50 per person, which most captains added into the price of the fare.

In 1882, the Supreme Court stated that this tax was unconstitutional, and as a result federal authorities took over the administration of Ellis Island from the City of New York. Another motive for this change was to curb the increasing corruption and exploitation of immigrants. The reception process had to be made more efficient as well because at the time more than 550,000 people were arriving annually.

Ellis Island During the Peak Period (1892-1916)

In many ways conditions improved on the little island next to the Statue of Liberty, though not all immigrants experienced it as such. "The Island of Tears", "a cross between Alcatraz and Devil's Island (two famous prison islands)" and other similar descriptions expressed the violent emotions and anxieties present in people who were arriving after weeks or even months of journeying.

Expectations and hopes were mixed with the fear of being turned away or perhaps cut off from family and friends. Most of their worries, however, were unnecessary. Of the 16 million people registered between 1892 and 1916, 80 % passed through directly and 20 % had to undergo a more thorough examination. Only 1 or 2 % were turned away (about 250,000 in all), mostly because they had tuberculosis or other contagious diseases such as trachoma, (an eye disease). Contract work was another essential reason for turning away immigrants. From the beginning of the 1880s, immigrants whose fares were paid in their homelands and who had signed a contract of work there might be looked upon as potential scabs and a threat against organized labor. The growing trade unions had forced this provision in the law. There are many examples of entire boatloads of cheap Mediterranean laborers being brought over in order to depress wages. This restriction also affected many individual immigrants.

The Immigration Act of 1882 was mainly directed against one group in particular: the Chinese. It halted all immigration from China. Thousands of Chinese had laid with bitter strength (the word "Coolie" means "bitter strength") the rails across the hazardous mountains and prairies under inhuman conditions for inhuman wages due to contract work.

The other major group of railroad workers, the Irish, organized themselves and supported the trade unions in all their safety regulations. To exclude an immigrant on the basis of contract work was difficult to administer. One immigration official put it this way: "If they come here without having a job and thus unable to support themselves, we have to turn them away. And now we also have to turn them away if they have a piece of paper proving that they have a job."

The bureaucracy was enormous and treatment was often superficial, depending on the inspector. But all things considered, the tragedies were few and far between. Of course this did not make matters any easier to understand for those involved in such tragedies. It might seem cruel and insignificant when authorities split up a family by allowing parents and some children to enter while turning away a child of twelve, but this was the law. Officials regarded twelve-year-olds as adults and could force them to return unaccompanied. Children under twelve were at least allowed to be taken home by a member of the family. The return expenses were paid by the shipping company that had brought them over. Although infrequent, these kinds of absurdities created all sorts of tension and anxiety among the immigrants. Many went through the formalities in less than an hour, but for most of them it took between three to six hours, according to how busy things were. During some years when more than one million passed through, it was common to admit 5-6,000 people on certain days.

Investigations and examinations then had the routine characteristics of an assembly line. The immigrants moved forward in long lines, in and out of booths, up and down stairs. All this moving about was part of the control and everything was strictly supervised. The steep stairs revealed difficulties in breathing, thus disclosing possible lung diseases. Everybody over two years of age had to walk alone. They had to carry their hand luggage unless it was too heavy because that might conceal a limp or some other disease or ailment.

The lines passed by doctors who quickly determined what further examinations, if any, were necessary for either treatment or rejection.

Many felt that they were being herded like so much cattle. They were pushed onward, bearing labels or chalk marks directly on their clothing. There were long lines, lots of waiting and then suddenly onward again.

"What's your name? Which ship were you on? What nationality? Where do you come from? Where are you going? Do you have any education? Do you have any skills? Who paid for your ticket? Can you read and write your own language? Do you speak English? How much money do you have? Are you suffering from any special diseases? What are your political convictions?" etc. Officials went through a set list of 32 questions in a couple of minutes and then shouted, "Next."

There were many problems with language and an overall tension which increased the confusion. Generally the inspectors were tolerant and very adept at making themselves understood, but even their patience wore thin now and then.

Most problems were solved and most questions answered – some even with a bit of humor. Names were a constant puzzle, and thousands of people left Ellis Island with another name than the one they entered with. Spelling and pronunciation were often complex so names were usually spelled in a hurried, pragmatic American way. A German Jew was so confused that when asked his name he replied, "Ik vergessen (I have forgotten)." The inspector then followed with, "Welcome to America, Ike Fergusson. Next!"

Of course only 2nd- and 3rd-class passengers had to go through immigration control. 1st-class passengers were presumed to be in good health and sufficiently well-off, so why bother them with trivial formalities? Welcome to God's own country where everybody is free and equal. Very few Danes were turned away. The reason for this can be found in the Emigration Act which was passed in Denmark in 1868, the main purpose of which was to protect the immigrants against harm and exploitation during the crossing.

Under the supervision of the Danish police, every passenger signed a contract. Sanitary conditions on board the ship had to be in order, as did the health of the emigrants. Therefore most of the Danes underwent thorough physical examination before they departed. Only a small number left Denmark because of religious or political persecution, and for that reason their con-

victions were rarely grounds for rejection. Many other nationalities had far more serious political and religious conflicts, so sending them back might have meant a prison term or execution. This may explain the approximately 3,000 suicides committed on the "Island of Tears", a gloomy statistic which speaks for itself.

The Immigration Act of 1882, directed primarily at the Chinese, led to a series of laws calling for broader restrictions: prostitutes, illiterates and left-wing people, particularly anarchists, were denied admission. Nobody under 16 years of age was allowed in without an older companion. The list of barring diseases grew and grew; the mentally ill, poor people who had been to jail or anyone deemed to be a burden on society were rejected.

In 1921 and 1924 the laws calling for quotas were introduced. These laws specified the number of immigrants to be admitted from each country. To Scandinavia this meant that the stream of immigrants now turned to Canada, Australia and South America, particularly Brazil and Argentina.

After World War II immigration and visa control were handed over to U.S. embassies in the countries of origin, and Ellis Island completed its role as the hub of U.S. immigration. During World War II the island served as a detention camp for "suspicious aliens", and during the McCarthy era of the 1950s it housed those who were suspected of "un-American activities". In 1954 the island was abandoned.

In 1985 plans have been announced for renovating Ellis Island into a museum.

The circular building, a former circus and fortress, Castle Garden, on the south of Manhattan was used as official immigration control from 1855-1892.

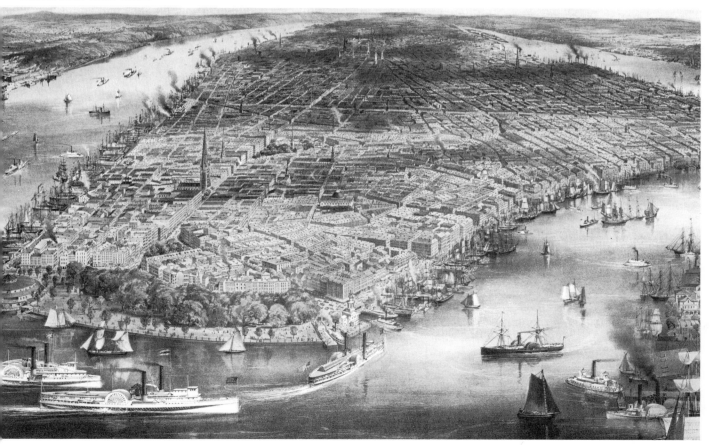

DREAM AND REALITY.

Since the arrival of the first colonialists America has had a fascinating effect on the Europeans – why?

What kind of America did the immigrants find when they came in droves in the period between the end of the Civil War in 1865 and the beginning of World War I in 1914?

Land of Freedom

"We shall be a City on a Hill, and the World shall look upon us"! As early as in 1631 when he founded Massachussets, the Englishman John Winthrop was convinced that any settling in the new world would cause excitement and interest in the old. And it is hardly a coincidence that Thomas More wrote his famous "Utopia" only some 20 years after Columbus had discovered America. Many of the tales from this new continent inspired the fantasies of a perfect society – Utopia – and for a long period of time America was the subject of many Utopian dreams of a better life.

The image of America as a land of freedom was created as early as the 1620s by the Pilgrims, and it was emphasized even more when the Declaration of Independence confirmed human rights and the ideals of freedom and equality in 1776.

This new land, where democracy and freedom of speech were not only in the minds of theorists, also caused great interest among the Europeans who did not care for the absolute monarchies of the old world. Even as far away as Denmark, tales from the American Declaration of Independence were used in the political debates caused by the French revolution in the 1790s.

Although not much was heard about America in the first half of the 19th century, this period gave rise to the most familiar image of America as not only the land of freedom and equality, but also the land of opportunity.

Chr. Winther wrote in his poem "The Flight to America" in 1835:

But if the ship gets across to the shore
it's a venture you'll never regret;
they'll give you a palace with horses and more
and mountains of money you'll get.

Liberty is just where you are at
to whatever you ever desire –
you spit on the floors when you feel like that
and play with cigars and fire.

The Danish public, however, did not start discussions about America until the 1850s and 60s when immigration really picked up, some 20 years after it had begun in the other Scandinavian countries. In these often heated discussions about whether it was "useful and good to emigrate to America", opinions often conflicted concerning American society.

The artist A. Smidt's reproduction of Peter's America visions from Chr. Winther's poem „The Flight to America".

Gold fever

"Gold is a wonderful thing! Whoever owns it is lord of all he wants. With gold it is even possible to open for souls the way to paradise!"
Christopher Columbus, letter to Isabella and Ferdinand, 1503.

"Later, I learned that Pahuska (the white men) had found there much of the yellow metal that makes the Wasi'chu (the greedy ones) crazy."
Black Elk, on United States Army expedition to Black Hills, 1874.

In January 1848 Swiss-born rancher John Sutter was building a saw-mill on the south fork of the American River in Northern California. He owned vast areas of woodland, and he intended to float the timber to Sacramento city further down the stream. When a canal was being constructed for the mill, however, considerable amounts of gold was washed out of the sand. Although Sutter tried to keep it a secret, the magic word „gold" raced like a fire across America, and reached Europe. The following year the Fortyniners came pouring in.

It cannot be stated how many Danes joined the race, but several letters indicate Danish participation with considerable success. One of these letters was written by a young miller from Jutland, Jens Storm Schmidt, who had emigrated in 1847 and settled in Texas. He joined the Gold Rush in March 1850.

„Dear Parents and Family. Finally, I have come back to civilization. That is, I am in a populated place where it is possible to mail a letter to you, all my dear ones at home. I sold my property and everything else in Texas for one tenth of what it was worth, bought 3 horses, rode on one, packed the other two. I had decided to travel overland to California.

I left my home on March 6, 1849, well equipped with pistols and guns, food and clothes, all that my horses could carry. For some days I rode alone, then I got company, some people from *Nye York*, and we travelled together to St. Antonio. When we got there nearly half the population had died from Cholera Morbus, and more died every day. But that was not all: a Mexican came into town with the news that Indians had killed six of his fellow countrymen and he was the only survivor; it happened 100 miles away, on my planned route. My companions then decided to turn back, and I was now alone. What could I do? Staying in the town and catch cholera would be worse than travelling through Indian country!

In the beginning I travelled in the day-time. When I was almost at the site of the murders I went deep into the forest during the day and by nightfall I mounted and rode on. During one of my nightly walks I suddenly came upon a place with an enormously bad smell. By the light of the moon I saw small heaps of embers. Can you imagine what this was: the site of the murders. You may imagine how I felt. But no more about that ... I travelled on. ...

... Arriving in *Sakramento-Town* my first question was how far it was to the gold mines; they said 30 miles. I walked around in mud to the knees to have a look at this one-year-old town just after the flood water had receded and returned to the old river bed. For the town is situated on the river carrying the same name, about 60-70 miles from *St. Frandsisko,* and now is a town of more than 4,000. The river overflowed its banks, flooding almost the whole town. When I speak about the population I speak of men, for I do think there are no more than 100 ladies in the whole town, and it is the same way all over the country: No women-folk except for a few yellow mexicans and red Indians.

Subsequently I bought the necessary food and provisions, built myself a gold-machine – which is not unlike a cradle – loaded my pack-horses and was off. When I got there I saw a number of people wriggling their machines, and I watched them for a while. The place is ugly, small and big stones have been thrown aside, under them is some red soil which you put in your bucket and carry to your machine which must be close to the water. Allright. I put up my tent to start out in my new trade. Golddigger. Ha, ha, ha – who would have imagined me as a golddigger! I tried the first day without finding anything. I got a little the next day, a little again the following day, but on the whole not much the first week. The next week I worked 4½ days, the rest of the time rain, and made 240 rix-dollars, good for a beginner. It made me more keen on working on these big stones and I have no doubt that when the river's water level falls I can make 30-40 rix-dollars a day.

And there we were, people from all corners of the world, even Chinese are here. People of all professions and crafts, generals, colonels, priests many of whom have put the book on the shelf probably because they feel that people do

not have the time to listen to them anyway, merchants, traders, captains, in short all kinds. If there is freedom and equality anywhere in the world it is here."

The Danish adventurer ended his letter here, but later added a post scriptum describing the world of the gold-digger:

„Since I first wrote I had a fight which I will tell you about for the fun of it. The day after I wrote I was beginning as usual digging for gold when an American came up to me, watched me and asked how much I was finding and was told so. He began digging a hole about 12 feet from mine according to the rules, then worked in the direction away from me, but found nothing. Then he comes up to me, looks at what I am finding, then goes back to his hole and works in the direction toward me. I went up to him and said he could not do that. He said he would dig where he pleased without asking since I had no right to dig at all (for there is a law saying that only American citizens are entitled to dig). I decided to tell him a thing or two about me having no right, and he decided to tell me a few things. We clashed. A moment later I was on top of him, and when he called for help a lot of people came running and separated us.

The men who had been on the site longest got together, saw what had caused the trouble and ruled that he had been asking for it. But that did not please him at all, he said I had struck the first blow and then crossed to the opposite river bank where he lived to send for three law officers who came to haul me before a court usually held in the middle of a field or in a tent with the invariable result that you pay the sheriff well for his trouble and that is all; it is not worth one iota.

At that time I knew almost noone except my old captain who swore that however many they were he would shoot them all if they touched me. But now I found many more friends and they all came up saying that they could not get at me unless they had a whole company big enough to beat them all and take me by force. They realized there was nothing they could do and left me alone. Now my neighbor has two loaded pistols lying beside him, and I have two, but mine have 12 – twelve – bullets. Don't think that I am a rowdy, but the law here is not strong enough to help a man have justice. And if you are a coward and cannot defend your rights you have no rights".

Peter Lassen of California

The Gold Rush came to an end – and so did the adventure of John Sutter. He was ruined in the mid-1850s and moved East, to spend the rest of his life in poverty in a German settlement in Pennsylvania. One of Sutter's neighbors and fellowpioneers in colonizing California did not find much gold, – though it might as well have been found on *his* land – but he came to play a far more important role in Californian history. He was a Dane named Peter Lassen.

Already in 1840 had this Danish blacksmith set foot on what was then Mexican soil in Northern California, and he became a great colonizer, founding settlements, cultivating the land, and at the same time acquiring fame as a protector of the local Indian tribes. He also protected nature – was an „early ecologist". He was widely respected among white settlers and Indians alike, and it was deeply ironic that he was killed by some Indians in the Honey Lake Valley in 1859.

In memory of his achievements as a colonizer a county and a national park bordering on Oregon bear his name, and numerous geographic sites are named after him. Among these is one of America's few active volcanoes, Mount Lassen; quite symbolic of this dynamic Dane.

Portrait of Peter Lassen from The Hesperian Magazine, San Francisco. The drawing is said to be based on a photography from ab. 1855, which has now disappeared.

Drawings from Colton: Three Years in California. The early gold-diggers carried their simple tools on their backs. Sometimes they were in luck!

48

The Conquering of the Continent

What had happened to this society since the colonies achieved independence from England in 1783?

The most obvious result was the immense increase in territory. The Mississippi River was reached as early as around 1800 and in 1804 The Lewis-Clark expedition reached the Pacific, and the trappers and gold-diggers sought their fortune in the Rockies. In 1849 the father of My Darling Clementine and other 49ers set off on their great gold rush which led to a rapid population growth in California. This territory, colonized by Spain, along with the territory north of the Rio Grande, had been taken in the war with Mexico from 1846-48.

At the same time, huge Mormon caravans rolled across the prairie in the 1840s towards the Great Salt Lake in Utah, while other pioneers battled through the wilderness to the fertile valleys of Oregon.

In 1861 at the beginning of the Civil War, the huge area from the Mississippi to the Rockies, the prairie, was still virgin land. Most of the remnants of the North American Indians occupied this region. They had been ruthlessly removed from areas previously settled by Europeans and they were given brief respite by the conflict which threatened to tear apart the United States in 1861-65.

Europe generally sees the American Civil War as the struggle of the Northern States to abolish slavery.

There were, however, other very poignant economic and political contrasts between the North and the South. But to Europeans the victory of the North and the abolition of slavery signalled a new confirmation of the U.S. as the land of freedom.

The years after 1865 saw an economic development which greatly increased the availability of material goods. This, too, served to make America all the more attractive to the old world.

The Making of an Industrial Society

The end of the Civil War in 1865 also signalled the beginning of the industrial revolution which made the U.S. the uncontested world leader before the turn of the century.

	1870	1910
Iron production	2 mill. tons	30 mill. tons
Coal production	20 mill. tons	417 mill. tons
Railroad net	34,000 miles	217,000 miles

Along with this quantitative growth, the U.S. experienced amazing advances in technology. Graham Bell's telephone and Edison's numerous inventions in the glow of his own light bulb revolutionized everyday life. The Wright brothers' 59 second flight heralded the era of aviation and in 1908 Henry Ford put his first automobile on the market. Five years later he introduced the assembly line which greatly reduced costs and thus made the automobile more affordable.

While technological advances increased industrial output, they also had a major impact on agriculture. During the years 1865-90, vast areas of prairie were converted into farm land. Modern farm equipment contributed to the doubling of cultivated areas as well as the tripling of corn, wheat and cotton production from 1870 to 1910.

A daguerrotype from 1850 of prospectors swarming around one of the Californian gold finds: men, women and children.

US growth from 1783-1912. The map reveals how the prairie and desert territories of the South West were last populated and accepted in the Union.

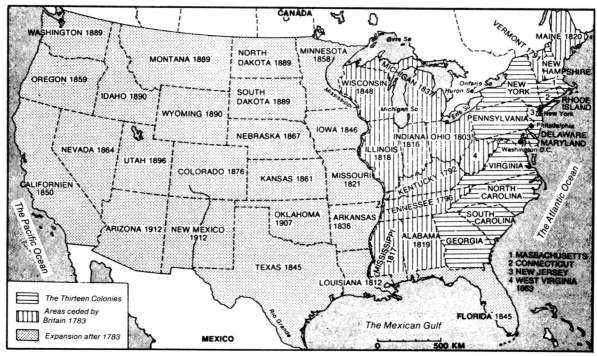

Henry Ford introduced assembly lines in Detroit 1913. 14 hours' work was reduced to 93 minutes.

What caused such enormous growth?

Apart from natural resources, such as tillable land, coal, minerals, etc. and improved technology, the most important factor by far was an immense growth in population – to which Denmark made a slight contribution. In 1860 the U.S. had 31 million inhabitants. By 1920 that number had increased to 106 million, more than a tripling within a time span of 60 years. To some degree this was due to an increase in the birthrate, but was mainly because 25 million Europeans immigrated into the U.S. during this period. The majority settled down in the cities east of Mississippi, particularly in New York and Chicago. These cities doubled in population several times. (New York went from 1 million in 1870 to 4,7 million in 1910). Statistics serve to bear out the notion that the U.S. was a "giant society in the making". An agricultural society became an industrial society, a society of villages turned into a society of big cities with all the consequences rapid urban growth entails in the way of slums and social problems. However, it also meant a ten-fold increase in the Gross National Product to be divided among a population that had only tripled.

It was normal for this development to take place with little interference from the government. Private enterprise was at the leading edge of progress – for better or worse.

America was the country in which each individual was the master of his own destiny. This was the ideal which continued to lure many millions across the Atlantic and the Pacific to the States. The prospects of going from rags to riches, from paperboy to tycoon were hardly as great as the prospects of winding up an underpaid worker in the slums of New York or Chicago. The pictures of the Danish reporter Jacob A. Riis from Manhattan's compact blocks with overcrowded apartments and tenements better represent the conditions in which European immigrants found themselves that the massive skyscrapers which served as a focal point for the eyes of Europe.

Big Bosses

Let us examine how this "society in the making" was being organized and run. During the years preceding the turn of the century, the developments in the world of business were marked by speculation and mergers, which served to concentrate more and more capital in the hands of fewer people.

It all started with the competion for the railroads; an intense fight went on, often using dirty business tactics to gain control of the dense net of railroads east of Mississippi. The railroad companies provided the resources to meet this fight through their monopoly in the West. Here the owners of the five transcontinental railroads, built in 1865-90, exacted exorbitant shipping rates, much to the dismay of the prairie farmers.

The monopolies reached their climax with Rockefeller's Standard Oil and Andrew Carnegie's United States Steel in the 1880s and 90s. These corporations were organized into so-called "trusts", i.e. the shareholders trusted their influence to a board who then made all the decisions. The shareholders then received their share of the profit.

A lot of political unrest arose concerning trusts and their leaders (then called "tycoons" or "moguls") claiming that this huge financial con- centration might be turned to political abuse. Despite repeated attempts, the everchanging governments were unable to break up these trusts until around the turn of the century.

In 1902 Teddy Roosevelt launched his attack which eventually led to the break-up of Standard Oil, and won Roosevelt his nick-name "the trust-buster". Nevertheless, the concentration of capital continued, though more discreetly, to dominate American economy.

A Trade Union Divided

Although there was a strong concentration of power and influence among the capitalists, it was apparently not possible for workers to organize themselves in order to increase their share of the profits. After the Civil War, America saw various attempts at forming trade unions, the most successfull of which were the Knights of Labor, a socialist organization of workers, which by the 1880s had 700.000 members. After 1886, however, the American Federation of Labor (AFL) surpassed it. The AFL distinguished itself from the Knights of Labor in that its membership was drawn from the ranks of skilled workers only, and that by charter its operations were strictly non-political. The purpose of the AFL was to improve working conditions and wages, while working exclusively within the existing economic and political frame-work.

This policy made AFL leader Samuel Gompers a very popular figure among the capitalists. By 1910 the AFL had acquired 1,5 million members, which was not too impressive considering the work force numbered around 35 million. They had no significant results to boast of either. This state of affairs was highlighted by severe defeats in the labor conflicts during the 1880s and 90s. But the labor movement faced great obstacles: the above disagreement concerning political goals, the exclusivity of the AFL, and finally the huge stream of cheap labor constantly pouring into the American work force from European ships. No wonder an important item on the AFL platform was to stop immigration. In a propagan-

Stockjobbers in Wall Street 1903
– and Children in Mullin's alley 1889.

da campaign with clearly nationalistic and racist overtones, they succeeded in stopping Chinese immigration as early as 1882, but not until the 1920s did the AFL win support for controlling European immigration. The 1924 Law of Quotas effectively brought the influx of excess labor to a halt.

Parties and Politics

The political system which set the groundwork for America's economic break-throughs was largely based on the system created by the Founding Fathers in the 1780s. During elections the two parties, Republicans and Democrats competed for the presidency and seats in Congress. It is very difficult to give a precise definition of the two parties; each covered broad areas of the political spectrum, and with all their complexities very hard to label. Just as today, the platforms then were frequently dominated by current is-

sues and by individual political personalities, rather than by ideological positions. Certain key issues and general principles, however, may be identified. After the North won the Civil War, the Republicans came to play a role in government until World War I, losing only two presidential elections before 1912. The party was formed in 1854 as a coalition of abolitionists and unionists, and after the Civil War, their policy was primarily that of confrontation with the "rebellious" South and with a strong emphasis on *national* policy. The presidential nominees were typically of national fame – heroes from the Civil War were among the preferred candidates – while local social and cultural conflicts were kept low-key. The Party pursued a protectionist policy with heavy tariffs on foreign imports, and a very liberal domestic policy which favored big business. Foreign policy came to be dominated by a strong nationalism which came to a head by the turn of the century. Proponents of this so-called "New American Imperialism" directed a foreign policy which precipitated the war with Spain in 1898.

For a long time the Democrats fought the stigma of being identified with the South and its cause in the Civil War. But when the war became history, it was clear that apart from having firm roots in the South, the party also attracted adherents among the vast groups of immigrants in the North by adressing local social and cultural conflicts. Just as today, the Democrats were the party for minorities, and increasingly they represented the interests of wage-earners and consumers.

These two old parties were not totally without competition. Time and time again a third party was established amid protest movements as an alternative to the existing system. The farm crisis in the 1880s produced a strong populistic movement, particularly among farmers in the West and the South. This movement won land-slide victories in parts of certain states from 1888 to 1896. Rooted firmly in the urban middle-class, the progressive movement established its own party in 1912 as a protest against growing political corruption.

Neither of these, nor the less important socialist movement gained broad support, however. The corruption and scandalous accounts of top people in the system might have shaken upon the Capitol or the White House but did not effect a change in the powerstructure. The alliance between big business and the established parties was too strong.

John D. Rockefeller, 1839-1937, the son of a miracle man who made billions in the oil business. He was right on the spot when the oil wells first sprang in Pennsylvania in 1859; he founded Standard Oil in 1870 and had complete control over the market through his trust from 1882 to 1911, when it was broken up into a number of small corporations. Rockefeller kept the control, he still made millions which he now, as an old man, spent on charity: research within medicine, development of the health service, museums and libraries.

Andrew Carnegie 1837-1919. He was the American dream personified: the poor Scottish boy who started as a messenger boy in Pittsburgh and ended having full control of the American steel industry through investments in the railroads. From 1873 to 1900 he created United States Steel, which he sold to the financier J.P. Morgan in 1902. He, too, spent many millions on charity: peace work, science and education.

Return to the Myth

In describing the U.S. in terms of the immigrants who arrived during the period between the Civil War and World War I, we have concentrated mainly on the changes in society.

These changes hardly altered the European concept of America, but they rather reinforced her image as the land of freedom and opportunity. To most of the immigrants the Statue of Liberty was the embodiment of their expectations. The joke that she turns her back on the States and stares longingly towards Europe came much later. The European debate was critical of the U.S., however, revealing a condescending attitude to this political upstart, this society with neither history nor tradition, and above all with *no culture.*

Was it anything else but a conglomeration of Europeans – not even first class citizens who happened to be thrown together, and could any good at all spring from this multinational melting pot?

Towards the turn of the century this problem became increasingly important to Americans. Did the country have any identity at all? Could one talk of an American nation? Any debate in the U.S. must be looked upon in light of this widespread change in all aspects of the country. In 1860 it was "a house divided", politically torn by the Civil War and geographically divided by vast, unpopulated areas in the heart of the continent. In 1900 it was marked by political stability, economic strength and after the last prairie states had joined the union it was a continuous, populated territory. On top of this she was ready to interfere in matters outside the American continent for the first time in her history.

This world power could not have been rooted in European heritage only, nor was it merely the result of a melding of groups who differed in culture and nationality.

This was at least the theory put forth by Frederick Jackson Turner in 1893 which has had a major influence regarding the way history is analyzed, as well as setting the tone for ideological debates in the U.S.

Turner maintains that the brutal Frontier life, where civilization and wilderness met, had had a deep effect on American culture and worldviews. Here life had created political attitudes, and mental and physical properties which distinguished an American from a European. The Frontier, as he called it, had been in Turner's days the vast prairies between the Mississippi River and the Rocky Mountains. The powerful images of the Old West that influence the perceptions of America at home and abroad were as universal then as they are today. One must admit that this concept would be impossible to repress.

Even today the "Frontier Theory" is crucial for American self-knowledge and the search for a national identity. Danish immigrants on the prairies of Nebraska were among those who inspired Turner's ideas. This theory has since been used to account for "political cowboys" who staked their claims on the herds of voters in the cities rather than on the long-horns of the prairie.

Ronald Reagan, President 1981, created his Western image as a film actor in Hollywood in the 30s and 40s.

Throughout this century to be associated with these ideas has proven successful – from Teddy Roosevelt to Ronald Reagan.

But let us not be dazzled by the charming simplicity of the Old West. America for the immigrant was not only a "little house on the prairie" or a great opportunity for the individual. It was also the slums on the East-side of Manhattan, and the desolation and misery therein. Although America was the leader in liberty and democracy, racism and political corruption were also found in the land of the Star Spangled Banner.

Very often the immigrant's dream of Utopia was a far cry from the harsh reality of the industrial worker or the prairie farmer.

Theodore Roosevelt, President from 1901 to 1909, created his Western image by acquiring a ranch and living like a cowboy for a decade.

SETTLING THE PRAIRIE.

Even though the typical Danish immigrant is seen as a Pioneer farming his small plot on the Midwestern prairie, statistics show that the diffusion of Danish Immigrants throughout America was quite extensive. In this aspect the Danes differ greatly from the other Scandinavians: while 19.6 % of all Swedish immigrants and 28.6 % of all Norwegian immigrants in 1910 settled in Minnesota, only 10.4 % of all Danish immigrants settled in the state with the highest concentration of Danes, Iowa. Like the other Scandinavians, the Danes made their way westward along the frontier trails. In the 1840s and 50s they settled down in the forests of Wisconsin and Michigan. Here they came upon already-established Norwegian and Swedish settlemens.

The mid-1850s saw the beginning of Danish settlements in Iowa; the two main centers for incoming Danes were Elk Horn and Kimbalton, and Council Bluffs received a huge influx of Danish Mormons who had lost their faith during the strenuous journey from St. Louis, Missouri, to the "Zion of the West", Salt Lake, Utah.

Danish immigration into Minnesota accelerated with the establishment of two Grundtvigian settlements: Tyler (1884) and Askov (1905). During the 1880s the Danes made permanent settlements in other prairie states: Nebraska, Montana, and the Dakotas. A group of Danes from Wisconsin had founded Dannebrog, Nebraska already in 1871, and another group founded a cattle-ranching community, Dagmar, in Montana (1906).

A "dug-out" on a homestead in Nebraska, 1892. The most primitive stage of dug-outs is behind them. This house is dug into a hill with a front built of sods.

Many folk high schools and churches were built in these settlements. Grundtvig followers founded Grand View College in Des Moines, Iowa (1896), while in Blair, Nebraska, *the Indre Mission* (Inner Mission) founded Dana College (1886) which to this day takes great pride in its Danish heritage. The relocation of an entire Danish community was rare, unlike the Norwegians and Swedes, who often moved entire villages, even counties, to America. They built their settlements as carbon copies of the original community back home.

The Danish settlements follow a pattern. The immigrants from the islands went primarily to Wisconsin and Michigan while the Jutlanders were predominant in Nebraska, but this is largely due to the fact that Danish immigration from the islands began before immigration from Jutland.

Today most Danish-Americans live in California. Solvang is no doubt the best-known Danish community in the U.S. In 1911, three Danish clergymen bought land for the settlement as a result of a religious conflict within their congregations in the Midwest. They sold the land in plots to individual members of their congregations who followed them from the prairie. Atterdag College was founded there (1912), and its church (1928) was built in the style of a traditional Danish village church. In the 1940s, Solvang changed from an authentic Danish settlement into a tourist site for Los Angeles. It became a "typical Danish settlement", complete with half-timbered dwellings, Danish pastries and storks on the roofs.

It is a far cry from Nebraska's Danish pioneers in their sod houses to the costumed ice-creme vendors in California's imitation half-timbered houses. This contrast best demonstrates the assimilation of the Danish immigrant into the American mainstream.

One of the big goals in life: the dug-out is substituted by the wooden house. This house is built of machine-cut boards from the sawmill. The sod-house now functions as barn and cow-house. Nebraska 1892.

Farmers Go West

The settling of the prairie itself extending west of the Mississippi River took place in the 25 years following the American Civil War, 1865-90. Until then the territory had been inhabited by Indian tribes who lived off the innumerable bison. Up to the 1860s the prairie had meant nothing but an unpleasant and dangerous obstacle for pioneers on their way west toward California, Oregon and the Mormon center in Utah. Only one or two stage coach routes and the famous postal service, the pony express, regularly crossed the prairie.

Hazardous travel conditions rendered the transport of much-needed provisions to the prairie almost impossible, let alone the sale of their own products back east. On top of this they faced the most basic problem: the lack of water.

Rain was often scarce over long periods of time, and the subterranean water table was far beneath the surface.

The post-Civil War years saw a more thorough taming of the prairie due to a more extensive transportation network, progress in farming technology and legislative initiatives.

In the latter-half of the 1860s, the railroad companies began laying track from the East and West, respectively. In 1869, during a grand ceremony at Promontory, Utah, the last rail was secured by the driving of a golden spike. Four other transcontinental railroads were built before 1890. These lines, including numerous branches, made it possible for prairie communities to get provisions and to send their products to market.

Among the advances in farming technology were the steel plow which made it possible to break the hard prairie topsoil, and wind mills

which were used to tap the underground water supply. Furthermore a new method of cultivation, "dry farming", allowed optimal use of the sparse precipitation through special preparation of the surface. And finally in 1874, the barbed wire was invented; this was the farmers' most efficient weapon in their on-going battle with the large ranch-owners who let their cattle graze freely on "the open range".

The legislative initiative included the passing of the Homestead Act which entitled any American citizen to acquire up to 160 acres of government land (65 hectars). He was then allowed to settle the land, cultivate it, and after five years the homesteader gained full possession of the claim. It is evident that this offer of free land came to play a very decisive role in American propaganda to promote immigration, and it had a "pulling" effect on landless Danish farmers.

Where did the Danes settle?

	1850	1860	1870	1880	1890	1900
California.....	92	1.328	1.837	3.748	7.764	9.040
Illinois........	93	712	3.711	6.029	12.044	15.689
Iowa	19	661	2.827	6.901	15.519	17.012
Michigan	13	192	1.354	3.513	6.335	6.390
Minnesota....	1	170	1.910	6.071	14.133	16.299
Nebraska.....	–	–	1.129	4.511	14.345	12.531
New York.....	429	1.196	1.698	3.145	6.238	8.746
Pennsylvania .	97	234	561	945	2.010	2.531
Texas........	8	150	159	489	649	1.089
Utah	2	1.824	4.957	7.791	9.023	9.132
Washington ..	–	27	84	296	2.807	3.626
Wisconsin....	146	1.150	5.212	8.797	13.885	16.171

One Billion Acres Under Plow

The bill had an economic as well as a political aim: partly to cultivate the land, but also to establish a politically stable population consisting of independent farmers on medium-sized farms. A closer look at the settlement of the West reveals that the law never quite fulfilled its purpose. Although about 285 million acres were transferred to private ownership through the act, a lot of this land wound up in the hands of a few speculators, who found ways to circumvent the process. During the same period no less than 700 million acres were disposed of by the Fede-

ral Government in the following ways: donated to individual states for public purposes; sold for cash (as was the case concerning territories taken from the Native Americans); or handed over to the railroad companies as an incentive for their work. Wide belts – ranging from five to twenty miles on either side of the tracks were given to the companies; this area was larger than France and Germany combined. The companies sold lands at varying prices, depending on proximity to the rails: who wouldn't want to avoid the hazardous transport of products across impassable prairie lands down to the railroad, the lifeline to the major markets back east?

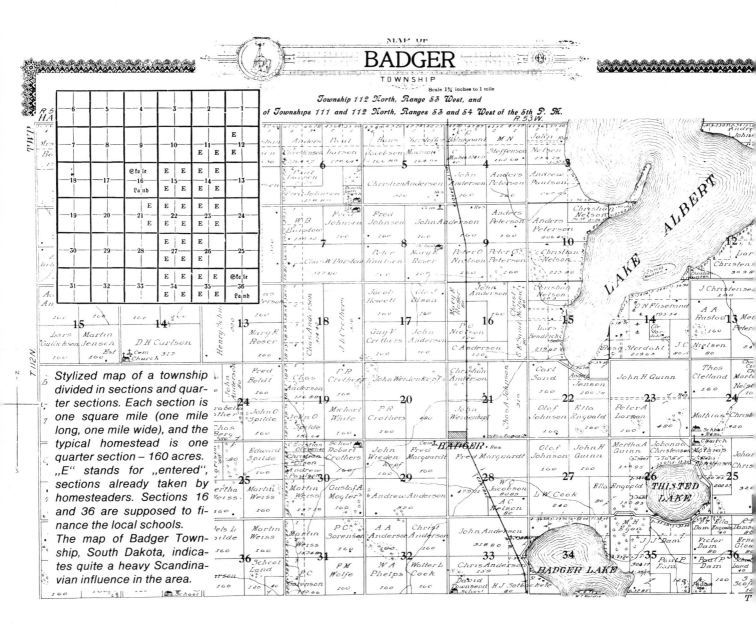

Stylized map of a township divided in sections and quarter sections. Each section is one square mile (one mile long, one mile wide), and the typical homestead is one quarter section – 160 acres. „E" stands for „entered", sections already taken by homesteaders. Sections 16 and 36 are supposed to finance the local schools. The map of Badger Township, South Dakota, indicates quite a heavy Scandinavian influence in the area.

Sod house from Custer County, Nebraska.

Slowly but surely Union Pacific workers toil through the hills. The need for human labor was huge: Central Pacific in the west employed Chinese and Japanese immigrants while Union Pacific in the east employed the Irish as well as the Civil War veterans, who joined the labor market after 1865.

The great day: the rails from Central and Union are united in Utah on May 10, 1869.

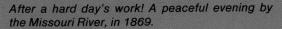
After a hard day's work! A peaceful evening by the Missouri River, in 1869.

The most important cattle trails and transcontinental railroad routes. The Northern Pacific received its lavish share of land grants.

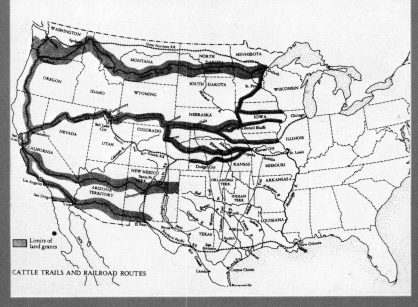
CATTLE TRAILS AND RAILROAD ROUTES

Homestead seekers at the land commissioner's office. The map over the plots is studied meticulously, while the settled gentlemen up front seem much more relaxed. Kansas, 1874.

RICH FARMING LANDS!

ON THE LINE OF THE

Union Pacific Railroad!

Located in the GREAT CENTRAL BELT of POPU-LATION, COMMERCE and WEALTH, and adjoining the WORLD'S HIGHWAY from OCEAN TO OCEAN.

12,000,000 ACRES!

3.000,000 Acres in Central and Eastern Nebraska, in the Platte Valley, now for sale!

We invite the attention of all parties seeking a HOME, to the LANDS offered for sale by this Company.

The Vast Quantity of Land from which to select, enables every one to secure such a location as he desires, suitable to any branch of farming or stock raising.

The Prices are Extremely Low. The amount of land owned by the Company is so large that they are determined to sell at the cheapest possible rates, ranging from $1.50 to $8.00 per acre.

The Terms of Payment are Easy. Ten years' credit at six per cent interest. A deduction of ten per cent for cash.

The Location is Central, along the 41st parallel, the favorite latitude of America. Equally well adapted to corn or wheat; free from the long, cold winters of the Northern, and the hot, unhealthy influences of the Southern states.

The Face of the Country is diversified with hill and dale, grain land and meadow, rich bottoms, low bluffs, and undulating tables, all covered with a thick growth of sweet nutritious grasses.

The Soil is a dark loam, slightly impregnated with lime, free from stone and gravel, and eminently adapted to grass, grain and root crops; the subsoil is usually light and porous, retaining moisture with wonderful tenacity.

The Climate is mild and healthful; the atmosphere dry and pure. Epidemic diseases never prevail; Fever and Ague are unknown. The greatest amount of rain falls between March and October. The Winters are dry with but little snow.

The Productions are wheat, corn, oats, barley, rye and root crops, and vegetables generally. Flax, sweet potatoes, sorghum, etc., etc., do well and yield largely.

Fruits, both Wild and Cultivated, do remarkably well. The freedom from frosts in May and September, in connection with the dry Winters and warm soil, renders this State eminently adapted to fruit culture.

Stock Raising in all its branches, is particularly profitable on the wide ranges of rich pasturage. Cattle and sheep

feed with avidity and fatten upon the nutritious grasses without grain; hogs thrive well, and wool growing is exceedingly remunerative.

Timber is found on the streams and grows rapidly.

Coal of excellent quality, exists in vast quantities on the line of the road in Wyoming, and is furnished to settlers at reduced rates.

Market Facilities are the best in the West; the great mining regions of Wyoming, Colorado, Utah and Nevada, are supplied by the farmers of Platte Valley.

The Title given the purchaser is absolute, in fee simple, and free from all incumbrances, derived directly from the United States.

Soldiers of the Late War are entitled to a Homestead of one hundred and sixty acres, within Railroad limits, which is equal to a bounty of $400.

Persons of Foreign Birth are also entitled to the benefits of the Free Homestead Law, on declaring their intentions of becoming citizens of the United States; this they may do immediately on their arrival in this country.

For Colonies, the lands on the line of the Union Pacific Railroad afford the best locations in the West.

TOWN LOTS FOR SALE VERY CHEAP in the most important towns on the line of the Road, affording excellent opportunities for business or investments.

Full information in regard to lands, prices, terms of sale, &c., together with pamphlets, circulars and maps, may be obtained from all the Agents of the Department, also the "PIONEER."

A handsome ILLUSTRATED PAPER, with maps, etc., and containing the HOMESTEAD LAW. Mailed free to all applicants. Address

O. F. DAVIS,
Land Commissioner, U. P. R. R.
OMAHA, NEB.

The railroad companies had good arguments for the superiority of their land: location, soil, climate and finances.

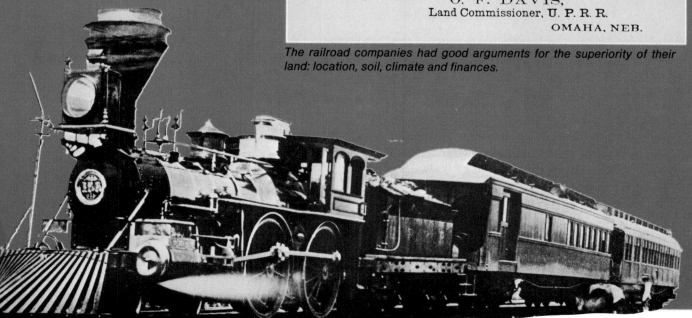

Life on the Homestead

What was it like for the pioneer who managed to get a homestead? Not only land was needed for starting a farm; it also called for seed, draft animals, tools and equipment, and housing. Apart from economic considerations, there were other problems such as the threat of Indian attacks, conflict with the ranchers who angrily watched barbed wire cross "their" grasslands and later controversies with the railroad companies which exploited the prairie farmer through their transportation monopoly. There were tasks to be undertaken, fights to be fought as well as sweat and toil to be endured before the homesteader saw his dream fulfilled.

His first task was to build a house. Wood houses were out of the question on the sparsely forested prairie. Other materials had to be found, or they had to make use of the possibilities offered by the landscape. Often the settlers simply built a dug-out into a hillside, if possible with a front door and a window.

Indeed the original dwelling on any homestead was more than likely a sod house. Often they consisted of more than one room. They varied in size; some even had a second story. Several years usually passed before the homesteader could afford a wood floor. A house built entirely of wood was a distant dream for the early pioneer on the prairie.

Sod for these dwellings was cut with a breaking plow in blocks that were two feet long and twelve inches wide, but only about 1½ inches deep. These sod bricks were piled about seven feet high. There were no boards for the roof, so instead they used small trees from the river banks with prairie grass thatched on top. The sod houses were warmer than wood buildings, but the roofs often leaked during a hard rain, and the floors became mud-puddles. Dugouts did, however, provide excellent protection against the heavy snows and brutal cold of winter. One major concern for the owner was keeping the animals off the roof: otherwise they might fall through and end up in the middle of the living room.

In most cases the settler worked the land for several years before making a profit. Areas from which sod was taken for the house were planted with wheat, corn and a vegetable garden. As soon as possible a couple of cows were acquired along with chickens and hogs. These animals and vegetables provided a certain security as far as a food supply during those first critical years.

Converting the homestead into productive farmland was a slow process, partly because a family could only clear about 30 acres per year, and partly because the man of the household often hired himself out as a hand on a nearby farm, a laborer in towns further away or a railroad worker. These were the only means to raise the necessary capital for seed and equipment.

During these early years the woman endured many hardships, not only because she had to do her share of the hard labor – she knew that from Denmark – but also because she was isolated and lonely. She lacked the security in living close to neighbors she knew and trusted. She gave birth under very primitive conditions. With children in the house, the pioneer woman had to work very long hours. Infants had to be fed and cared for. She had to bake, cook, tend to the house and provide clothes for her family as well. On top of all this she and the children had to be ready to lend a hand, whenever needed, especially during the harvest.

By being very meticulous in growing potatoes and vegetables in her garden, she provided a significant portion of the food needed to see her family through winter. When times were bad she often was the only one to provide even a meager income by raising chickens as well as selling eggs and butter which she churned from milk. When the harvest was complete, the accounts were settled, debts paid, and the profit, if any, was tabulated. Then they could determine what, if anything, they could afford to buy. Necessities came first: more and better oxen and horses for plowing, more cattle, equipment (e.g. a cart, a proper stove, building materials, etc.) Down the list of priorities came proper doors and windows for the sod house, floor boards, roof boards, a table and chairs, and finally, the sheer luxuries such as Sunday clothes, an oil cloth for the table and shoes for bare feet.

The rough beginning –
a dream fulfilled.

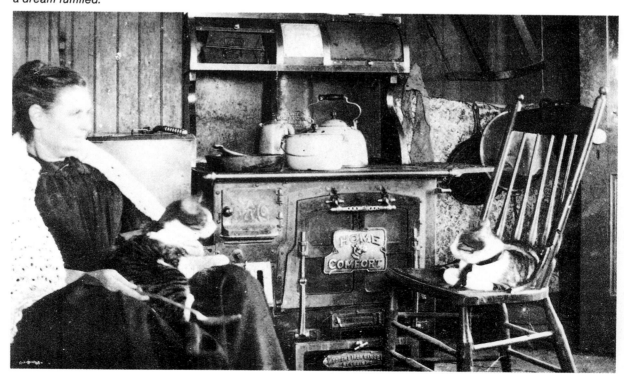

A Danish Settlement in Nebraska

One of the leading Danish reporters during this era, Henrik Cavling, travelled among the Danish pioneers in the Midwest in 1888, and in his book "From America" (1897) he describes the establishing of a Danish settlement on the Nebraska prairie.

"For many days the five Danish pioneers strove through badlands on which only Indians had set foot. After travelling for several weeks they reached the Loup River, which they could not cross without a bridge. They had to fetch material for this in Grand Island to the south. This took time, but Lars Hannibal felt that beyond that river they would find what they were looking for. Land reminiscent of their homeland. After numerous ordeals they crossed the river to the site where Dannebrog was founded. They dug into the topsoil and when they found mold covering clay they decided this was the place; these five impoverished men sat down on the bare ground and dreamt about a *Little Denmark*. In their minds they envisioned the *Dannebrog* flying over the territory, so they named the town after the flag."

They were Danish farmers from a Wisconsin settlement established in the 1840s, but had set out to claim new land further west.

"In the following year (1871), a caravan with women and children made its way there, and in Grand Island the farmers purchased deeds for the land at $ 14 per 160 acres ...

Slowly the prairie was broken, sod houses were upgraded with lumber, and eventually the

The Market Place „Kongens Nytorv", Dannebrog.

farmers built the painted wood houses, many of which can be seen even today. A mill was built and better machinery was bought. But not that many years beforehand, conditions were so primitive that the farmers had to ride for three days to get to a blacksmith when the plow-irons needed repair. Soon afterwards an astonishing development took place in all aspects of life. The Danish farmers gained access to excellent schools, banks and churches, and they had midwives and doctors (from Denmark and Germany), pharmacists and craftsmen. There were railroads, post offices and telegraph operators, so even though the price of grain went down, most of the farmers were well-off ...

The houses were made of wood and far too small for the extensive plots. The signs displayed Danish names, but apart from that nothing was typical of Denmark. As you walked past the

square along the main street, you came to the river, the town's side of which was lightly wooded and enclosed by a fence. Near the entrance there was written in big letters Central Park. As I later learned this was the town playground. Further down the main street there was a blacksmith, standing at his door and we started talking. Not far from the blacksmith we found the Hotel Dania, and above one of the neighboring houses there was a sign that said Star's Editorial Office.''

Progress, Problems and Protests

After the Danish farmers had endured the hard times and had learned to adjust to the American way of farming, they now lived more or less under the same conditions as the other American farmers. Farming in Dannebrog, however, entailed its own set problems. The farmers complained that the railroad-owners were sheer exploiters, robbing them beyond all belief. They found the freight charges far too high, and Danish farmers maintained that it was cheaper to send a pound of butter from Copenhagen to Chicago than from Dannebrog to Chicago. The exorbitant rates were due to the fact that the railroads exploited their monopoly in the West to counter losses east of Mississippi due to strong competition from the numerous other railroads.

The farmers also complained that they were exploited by middlemen who, while it was cheap, bought up grain, stored it, and sold it for a substantial profit later on. And finally they directed their anger toward the government and the banks, maintaining that the government was embarking on a deflationary policy by reducing the amount of money in circulation, thus leading to heavy slumps in the economy. As the interest rates on the farmers' mortgages became an increasing burden, they often had to go to the banks for support. According to the farmers, the banks took advantage of the situation and charged usurious interest rates.

All these problems gave rise to a protest movement in the Midwest and the subsequent forming of the Populist Party in 1892. Many Danish farmers were active in this movement. In many other ways, too, the Danes began to be integrated into American society – albeit slowly in the beginning and with a certain reserve.

The followers of Grundtvig tried to preserve their Danish heritage for as long as possible. Their children, growing up in America, felt like Americans, so they did not compare everything to Denmark. To many of the 3rd generation, Denmark was a country like any other on the map. Even those who ardently tried to stay ''Danish'' realized that it was only a matter of time until being a Dane was something for special occasions only. The church, the folk high schools and the brotherhoods were their gathering points.

This fight for the preservation of what was ''Danish'', and the debate as to whether it was a reasonable goal at all was evident in all Danish settlements – from the prairie villages in Nebraska to the streets of Chicago.

68

Women of the West

Bertha Joseph Anderson arrived with her family to Montana in 1889 where they settled down near Ft. Buford, and quickly realised that they could make a living by selling dairy products to the soldiers at Ft. Buford.

50 years later, in 1938, Bertha Joseph Anderson took the time to describe her life on the prairie, a life which was marked by hard labor, numerous childbirths and where they "grew to depend on the Lord first and common sense next." They started out by buying ten milk cows

"... paying down a little and signing notes for the rest. It was not the way I thought we should start, but Carl thought it was the only way, and he seemed to know. There was no way of starting to farm that spring."

They toiled through, and her memoirs constantly tell us about their tough life.

"It did not look any too good, but young people who are down to bedrock and have three small children and can't speak for themselves, can't give up even if they want to."

They eventually get ready for business and it is a very good thing that she had learned the dairy trade, because although her husband did his share, he never really got the hang of milking. Her memoirs give us a good impression of her industrious and hard life, when she describes the long working days:

"... as soon as the evening milking was done and a bite of supper eaten, I would start getting the butter ready. We had about one hundred pounds a week, and though it was all worked and put in big containers after churning, it had to be worked over again and put in one pound wooden molds. Then it was set on slats or boards in boxes, and placed on the platform of the buckboard, and then transported to the Fort.

I always had Peter go to bed as early as possible, as he couldn't help with that work. I spent the night getting the hundred pounds of butter ready. Usually I had finished by three or four o'clock in the morning. I then called Peter, got his breakfast, and he was off before five, as he had to be down at the Fort before it got warm, since we had no ice and the butter would melt. ... I then had my work cut out for me at home, milking twenty-three cows, carrying the milk to the

spring, skimming the milk and feeding the calves. It was nearly nine o'clock on Saturday mornings before I could get to the house to look after my children ... I never had a chance to be lonesome or homesick, for my hands were full of work from daylight until long after dark."

Bertha Joseph Anderson's life was similar to the majority of Danish immigrant women. Most of these women spent their lives toiling on farms, some successful, some just making it, and some failing and giving up.

Till now not much is known about the women in the cities. Some worked in sweatshops as seamstresses, some as shop assistants, but they do not seem to have written letters home to Denmark to the same degree as the women in the country, and research into their lives has been very sparse.

Some of those women in the cities fulfill the expectation we have of the American Dream, a dream of success and money. *Marie Mynster (1822-1893)* was in many ways the embodiment of the American Dream. She was married to Christopher O. Mynster, a silk merchant from Hillerød, and in 1842 they set out for America with their 4 year old son, William.

Bertha Anderson – 1943. Stars in window for nine grandsons who served in World War II.

Marie Mynster.

After living in Washington, D.C., for four years, her husband heard about the gold rush and the extensive Mormon trails and decided to seek his fortune in the West. In Kanesville, now Council Bluffs, Iowa, he invested in Mormon claims – so much so that the Mormons took him for a government agent who planned to buy them out. Two years later, however, he died of Spanish fever, leaving Marie a 30-year-old widow. She tried to get the claim on her husband's land, but "claim jumpers" cheated her out of a considerable part of it. Only by building a crudely timbered cabin and living in it for two years did she retain the rights to the land. She then took charge of her husband's business, both that of dry goods and of real estate. Whatever money she made, she invested in land and she laid out the Mynster addition to the city. In 1860 she secured the property known as Mynster Springs, one of the most beautiful spots in all Iowa. Later, in 1879, her son, William, erected a fish hatchery there and planned to make a popular resort of the area.

Mrs. Mynster had already built a handsome, Gothic-style family residence there near a beautiful spring whose waters were said to possess healing powers.

She did not socialize with other rich American families, such as the Dodges in Omaha, but led a very secluded life. She spent whatever spare time she had teaching her only son, and later her grandchildren, Danish which she herself still spoke as fluently as if she had never spoken any other language.

When she died at age 81, her estate amounted to $ 200,000. The fact that she changed the family name from Mønster to avoid being called "Monster" tells us that she also possessed a certain amount of self-irony.

Captain Maren Christiansen was responsible for the establishment of one of the largest homes for destitute women run by the Salvation Army in Cleveland, Ohio.

She was born the daughter of a well-known farmer in Vendsyssel. At age 15 she went to America to visit her ten(!) brothers. She liked the country and decided to stay. Four years later she came into contact with the Salvation Army, and through this organization she saw the opportunity to work for the common good of mankind. She soon became admired and respected, particularly for her love and understanding when helping destitute women, her more unfortunate sisters. She knew how to make the "haves" take an interest in the "have-nots", especially in her work among these women. But not only the rich took an interest; so did the local authorities who were very anxious to help her and to learn about her work. Judge Adams of the Juvenile Court in Cleveland helped her establish a temporary residence in the Salvation Army shelter for the young girls who were tried at the Juvenile Court, thus sparing them the brutalities of prison.

Captain Maren Christiansen.

Sincerely yours
C. Madsen

US MARSHAL MADSEN.

He was only 13 when he found his brother killed in the terrible war with Germany in 1864, when Slesvig in the Southern part of Denmark was lost. That was the beginning of a long violent life of a peace-loving man.

In America he was respected and feared as Chris Madsen, soldier and U.S. marshal.

Chris Madsen was the name he was given when he was born in 1851 in Slesvig, while it was still under Danish flag.

He lived an incredible life of action and drama, a life of a kind we normally only meet in fiction or on the silverscreen. To him it was reality.

Few others, if any, have lived to fight Bismarck at Dannevirke and Dybbøl in 1864 and lived long enough to fight "This ... Mr. Hitler..." in 1944.

In between he fought several wars in Europe, Africa and America, not because he was a violent man, rather the contrary. He fought with a strong and determined belief that everybody had a right to live in peace and after their own choice. He knew what he was fighting for, he knew the pain of losing family and country.

In the beginning revenge was part of his motive. He was only a kid when Slesvig was lost to Germany. That in itself led 50-60.000 people to emigrate, because they didn't want to live under German rule. The young Christian was marked during the final fight and the retreat on April 18th '64. He was separated from his father, who was wounded, and when he tried to escape across the bridge to Als he stumbled over the body of his older brother killed by German bombs.

A couple of years later he was sent to Copenhagen to become an officer, but after three years, service he, like many others, decided that the only chance to fight Germany and to get a fast promotion was to join a foreign army.

Sword Against Sword Without Mercy

France was preparing a war with Germany, so Christian Madsen enlisted in The French Foreign Legion in Africa for a five-year period. France lost the war and Madsen almost lost his life in the Battle of Sedan in 1871. He was taken captive and imprisoned close to his hometown. Fearing he would be recognized and shot as a traitor (since he was fighting against what was formally his own country) he managed to escape.

Chris Madsen. In uniform of Regimental Quarter master Sergeant of the First U.S. Volunteer Cavalry – "Rough Riders."

Teddy Roosevelt's regiment in the Spanish-American War. About 1899.

Fort Laramie, Wyoming.

He returned to the fighting only to find his regiment scattered, so he joined the Italian revolutionary Garibaldi, who had arrived to support the French.

After the French-German war he was sent back to Africa to fight the Arabs in Algeria, but war never showed any glory to him.

He did not renew his contract with the Legion. He left Africa but really had no place to go. In a sense he had lost both his homelands. In Slesvig he would face a trial and in Denmark he might fear an extradition. So he went to Norway where he worked with the whalers for a while, heavily handicapped by seasickness. He then spent the most of a year as a surveyor on the Westcoast around Bergen before he took the big decision.

Fighting Indians

"We were sent to Arizona for to fight
the Indians there
we were almost snatched bald-headed, but they
did not get our hair
we lay among the canyons and the dirty
yellow mud
but we seldom saw an onion or a turnip
or a spud."

(Old fighting song).

In the beginning of January 1876 he landed in New York unable to find work like the thousands of other unemployed immigrants. But there was one thing he knew: the trade of the soldier. January 21st he was enlisted in the later so famous 7th Cavalry led by General George A. Custer, who was preparing the "final" blow at the Indians in a summer campaign.

Madsen was sent West, but fortunately transferred to the Fifth Cavalry and so avoided Custer's tough luck at Little Big Horn. Almost. According to the official documents and the huge stone memorial at Custer Battlefield he *was* killed there. In 1927 he revisited the old places and saw his name on the stone. That hit him. Afterwards he stoicly decided that he had found the reason for his troubles getting his military pension. So he formally informed the War Department that he was alive, which they formally accepted. But it haunted him for the rest of his life. Recently we have found out that there were actually two Danes named Christian Madsen enlisted in the 7th Cavalry, and the other one did die on that 25th of June. But Madsen never knew.

For 15 years he rode with the Fighting Fifth and advanced to quartermaster sergeant participating in all the major Indian battles and campaigns including the hideous "hunger" march commanded by General Crook. He was a favored scout and hunter since he was the best marksman of the whole regiment.

"Slesvig, from you another noble son
was forced away from family and friend
forced in spite of mother's tears – he's gone
never will he se your soil again.

A silent sigh dissolved into the night
they closed his eyes and covered his head
a last Farewell to a life in fight
the soldier in a foreign land lay dead."

(From a song written by C.M. about a Danish comrade who died Christmas Eve in the field during an Indian campaign. Roughly translated by S.T.)

Buffalo Bill, one of the hired scouts and later a worldfamous showman, became a good friend of his and as a curiosity Madsen was one of the two reliable eyewittnesses to Buffalo Bill's much debated killing and scalping of the Cheyenne Yellow Hand (correctly Yellow Hair).

Madsen married Maggie Morris and took land in Oklahoma in the big "Run" of 1889. He decided that his wife and their son and daughter deserved a more quiet and secure life than that of the army, so he joined the ranks of the U.S. marshals (!) Anyway the pay was considerably better and offered more independence.

Miss Maggie B. Morris

Chris Madsen and the movie actor Roy Rogers in Hollywood 1942.

The Star

For 26 years he was one of the U.S. marshals that tried to bring law and order to the "wild west". He also became a single father bringing up the kids. Maggie died very young from pneumonia.

He left his job as a lawman for a little while, but only to accept an appointment to become one of the organizers of Teddy Roosevelt's Rough Riders, the voluntary regiment formed in 1898 in the Spanish-American war. He went with Roosevelt and General Woods when Cuba was invaded, but had to return when he got the feared "fever".

As a lawman he was a quiet, easygoing troubleshooter, and a crackshot to that. But he was far from what the myth-makers named him: "The Trigger-marshal".

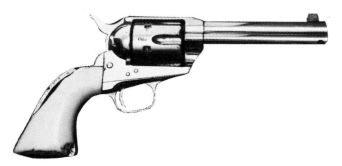

In spite of the thousands of arrests he made, he never killed a man. That is a clean record. He was respected and known to get what he went for. He would spend endless weeks in the tracks of criminals alone or as part of the most famous and efficient law and order team ever: The Three Guardsmen:

Bill Tilghman, Heck Thomas and Chris Madsen. They were the frontiermarshals that did the heavy work including (in-) famous outlaws as the Dalton-Doolins. He never touched alcohol, which in those days added to the reputation of a man of action.

In World War I he was offered the rank of major but he decided to decline. In stead his son Reno went as an engineer and fought at Sedan without getting wounded. During his lifetime Madsen fought the Indians, but also learned to respect, admire and later protect them. He became aware that their situation was so much like his own: a people defending their right to a homeland. He was formally "adopted" and made a "chief" of Whirlwind's Cheyenne's (the ceremonial pipe is still with his family) and he was a very close friend of Quanah Parker, to name two of the wellknown leaders. Quanah Parker in 1908 helped him, Tilghman and Thomas make what to day must be recognized as the first *real* western movie.

He was active until his death in 1944 but unfortunately he did not live long enough to see Hitler's downfall.

The last couple of years he spent writing his memoirs, an incredible source of pioneer history, that still has not been published.

This quote would be a proper epitaph for a man who devoted his life to freedom and fought for it. He ought to know what he is talking about:

"... and other nations will come to learn, that any country spending more billions on war materials than on schools, and educating more officers than teachers, is digging its own grave."

Chris Madsen

Chris Madsen at home in Guthrie, Oklahoma. Age 91.

HOKA HEY!

– it is a good day to die ...
... because it is a good day to live.

ON INDIAN LAND.

In 1869 the town of Denmark near the Spillman River in Lincoln County, Kansas, consisted of little more than a few log cabins and sod houses. On May 30 of that year this small community fell victim to a brutal attack by hostile Indian tribes. There were few survivors.

It was difficult for the prairie Indians to understand the pioneers' greed for land and material goods. They were free nomadic peoples who subsisted by hunting and bartering. They realized that these new settlers were powerful and that they had come to stay. While they might have to adjust to the pioneers' presence, the Indians believed that there was plenty of room everyone.

Unfortunately the U.S. government and the droves of immigrants who were lured into the open territories did not share this view. The settlers' goal was to acquire precious land – fertile and rich in gold and silver (as well as coal, oil, uranium and numerous other minerals to be extracted by succeeding generations). There were 371 treaties signed between the various sovereign nations and the United States. It is no exageration to state that the U.S. broke them all. It cannot be otherwise when two such totally different cultures clashed, especially when one is so much more powerful than the other.

The attack upon the small Danish settlement in Kansas was one of many such attacks on the settlers. The reason for these attacks may lie in the numerous attacks perpetrated by whites, be they soldiers or civilians. That aspect of history, however, is not to be treated here.

History recounts very few clashes between Danish settlers and the Native Americans they came in contact with, although descriptions of Indians are often found in letters, stories and articles. During the peak years of settlement (1850-90), the Indians were present throughout the prairie, either in person or as a potential danger. In Nebraska, settlements such as Dannebrog, Dannevang and Nysted were founded in the heart of the Pawnee territory, but on the whole their co-existence was peaceful.

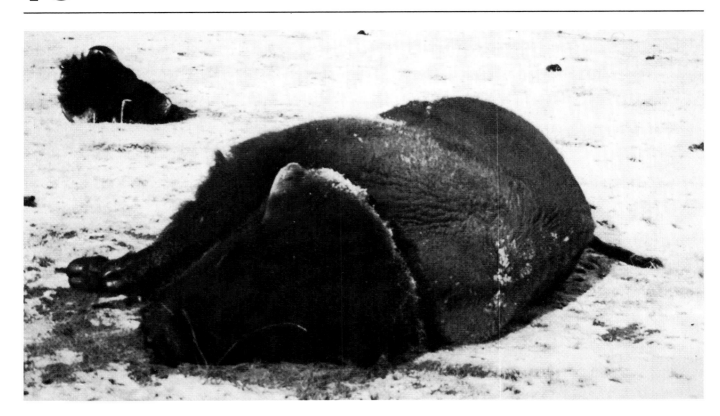

The Beginning of the Wars with the Indians, or How a Dane's Cow Came to Be a Threat to U.S. National Security

Single persons or single events alone do not make history, but they may touch off a major event, sometimes totally by chance. Take for example a tired old cow.

There were skirmishes and clashes between the Indians and the many white settlers from the moment the latter set foot on the American continent. But during the 1850s to the 1890s it was regular warfare with raids and massacres, even against Indian women and children. The California gold rush marked the beginning and the end came at Wounded Knee. These were the years of the Wars with the Indians, and battles were fought from the Mississippi River in the East to the Pacific Ocean in the West; from Canada in the North to Mexico in the South.

The settling of the West provoked these clashes and it was only a matter of time before the political powers realized their plans. In the beginning of the 1850s when the wagons rolled towards the West with hundreds of thousands of pioneers, settlers and prospectors, tensions between whites and Indians were mounting – like a stick of dynamite with a very short fuse.

It was pure chance that a Dane happened to light the fuse and thus start 50 years of warfare. It still makes an odd tale about the importance of the Danes in America, and to think that it all had to do with a cow so emaciated that it is unlikely that it would have reached the final destination.

In August, 1854, a wagon train of settlers was working its way towards Salt Lake City. They were Danish Mormons on their way to Zion (which later became Utah). They followed the Mormon Trail running close to Fort Laramie on the border of Nebraska and Wyoming. Unfortunately one of the cows was so exhausted that it strayed into the Brulé camp where it was quickly killed by High Forehead, one of the many Minneconjous visiting with their allies. This was the custom of the prairie: stray cattle were free game, be they wild or domesticated. If a certain Mr. Nielsen had not had such a temper and been so stubborn, this might have been settled peacefully. Instead he rushed to the garrison at Fort Laramie and demanded not only compensation, but also that the "Redskin" be arrested and punished.

If Lieutenant John L. Grattan – fresh from West Point – had not been such a trigger-happy hothead, a trader named Bordeau and the commander of the fort might have succeeded in securing the immigrant routes a little longer. Lt. Gratten set out on a punitive expedition against the Indians. The chief's generous offer of first one, then five of his best horses could not quench Nielsen's craving for revenge nor the lieutenant's dream of honor and glory in battle. His dream turned into a nightmare: he himself was killed with all his men and thus the cow had become a matter of national security. From then on history was directed mainly from the War Department in Washington, D.C.

They made us many promises,
more than I can remember,
but they never kept but one;
they promised to take our land,
and they took it.

mahpiua luta (Red Cloud) oglala lakota

The Indians are Forced to Retreat

President Andrew Jackson was one of the earliest and most ardent supporters of the deportation of Indians onto reservations, unless they could be conquered or removed by other means. In many ways his Fifth Annual Message to Congress, December 3, 1833, formed the basis for U.S. policy toward the Indians for the next hundred years.

"My original convictions upon this subject have been confirmed by the course of events for several years, and experience is every day adding to their strength. That those tribes can not exist surrounded by our settlements and in continual contact with our citizens is certain. They have neither the intelligence, the industry, the moral habits, nor the desire of improvement which are essential to any favorable change in their conditions. Established in the midst of another and a superior race, and without appreciating the causes of their inferiority or seeking to control them, they must necessarily yield to the force of circumstances and ere long disappear. Such had been their fate heretofore, and if it is to be averted – and it is – it can only be done by a general removal beyond our boundary and by the reorganization of their political system upon prin-

ciples adapted to the new relations in which they will be placed ..."

There is therefore an interesting discrepancy between popular beliefs about the Indians and the reality of the relations between them and the pioneers. They were mainly thought of as bloodthirsty, uncivilized savages who hindered progress and thus should rightfully be removed. In spite of their beautiful, ancient spiritual and religious traditions, they were accused of being "heathens" and "godless". This always legitimized the word of the missionaries and the use of the weapons that supported them.

Strong arguments were needed to remove those who had first claim on the land, and they were established no matter if they were true or not.

Very often the Danes were among the second or third wave of pioneers when mass immigration had already gathered momentum, so "we" can hardly be held responsible for the brutalities and outright genocide which took place. Nevertheless these acts were a prerequisite for a "free" country.

Sitting Bull was once asked what the Indians called the country before the arrival of the whites. Without hesitation he answered, "Ours."

We must all see
ourselves as part
of this earth, not
as an enemy from
the outside who
tries to impose
his will on it
we, who know
the meaning of
the pipe, also
know that, being
a living part of
the earth, we
cannot harm any
part of her
without hurting
ourselves

Lame Deer

From Old Lame Deer's last
instructions to his son
Archie Fire Lame Deer:

''Respect for mother Earth.
Respect for the Great Spirit.
Respect for Fellow Man.
Respect for individual freedom,
provided,
that individual freedom
does not threaten the people
or the tribe or mother Earth.
For those that misuse
these ancient prophicies
will be punished even
in this lifetime
called
the circle of life.''

SETTLING IN THE CITIES.

Around the 1890s there was a growing shortage of tillable land for the increasing number of immigrants. Apart from the Indian reservations, the entire prairie was by now under cultivation. The 1890 U.S. census stated briefly that "the frontier" had disappeared; the continent was settled. Increasingly the immigrants concentrated in the big industrial cities, and the U.S. experienced a huge migration from rural to urban areas in the later part of the century, particularly during the agricultural crises in the 1880s and 90s.

Unfortunately information is sparse about the life of the Danes in American cities. It is estimated that by around 1910 more Danes lived in the cities than in the country. Chicago was the biggest "Danish" city with about 10,000 Danish-born inhabitants.

Danish immigrants in sweatshops in Racine, Wisconsin. In the archives surprisingly few pictures are found from the workshops of the immigrants. Most of them even lack the most elementary datas. 90 % of the pictures preserved show men of the clergy and prominent characters within the Danish-American brotherhoods.

Information is lacking mainly because the Danes in the urban areas realized the importance of learning the language and adopting the American life-style much sooner than their rural counterparts. What might also have come into play was a change in the age of the immigrants: there were more young single people and fewer families.

Urban conditions resembled those which the farmers experienced on the prairie: the first period was marked by scarcity and thrift; progress followed slowly. When a young artisan or laborer arrived in Chicago, he could find a room in one of the numerous immigrant hotels unless relatives or other contacts awaited him. These hotels often worked as a kind of employment office: the employers showed up to hire workers. Otherwise the immigrant had to try to find work on his own, and although Chicago was frequently flooded with unemployed workers, the Danish immigrants usually found a job rather quickly. Many newcomers were employed in the construction industry where ¼ of the Danes worked. Others were employed in the slaughterhouses, various workshops or in trade.

The newly-arrived artisan often found it difficult to adjust to a new employment. Manners were different from those in Denmark, and the certificate which had previously provided status did not have the same value in America. This difference is vividly described by the Danish reporter, Henrik Cavling, later the chief editor of the leading Danish newspaper, *Politiken,* for 25 years. He revolutionized the Danish press, mainly inspired by his encounters with the American press. Around 1890 he travelled all over the U.S. gathering material on the Danish immigrants through interviews ant other personal contacts. Cavling writes:

"Before the worker leaves his home in the morning he has breakfast. At the shop he works from 7:00 to 12:00 without a break. After a half-hour lunch, the only break, he returns to work until 5:30 – a 10½ hour day. He neither eats nor drinks during the workday. Any man who brings a bottle of liquor will be fired immediately. If anyone

Danish-Americans seated at the famous „round table" from Wilken's basement bar in Chicago. In the center behind the table is Max Henius, whose name is closely connected to Chicago, and who was the founder of the Danish-American Society.

smells of liquor, perhaps consumed on the sly, he is looked upon as a drunkard, even by those who drink after quitting time. This very widespread contempt for liquor is probably the result of the Good Templars' and the Methodists' relentless fight against alcohol. In the workshop and on the building site the worker does not care about anybody but himself. He does not strike up conversation with his fellow workers, and he can work alongside them for a long time without ever knowing their names. The foreman is regarded as an equal, and the worker does not take off his hat to his superiors. The cringing European-type behavior creates antagonism in co-workers and superiors. Strict supervision guarantees that the work continues without delay, and laziness is invariably punished by dismissal. They work harder in the West than in the East, but even in the East a man has to work twice as hard as in Europe. Better tools and more pressure makes this possible. Sign painters in the U.S. are offered the same wages as in Denmark where they earn 3-4 Danish crowns per day. In America they make $ 3-4 per day, but they work four times as hard, and the quality of their work is – as far as I have been informed – certainly not poorer in America than in Copenhagen.

At home skilled workers are held in high esteem, but this is not true in America. A good beginner immediately gets higher wages and

The interior of a well-known saloon in the Danish Chicago settlement, Lagoni's (1898). Contemporary descriptions emphasize the social function of the saloon for the Danish workers. It was just as important as two other Danish-American strongholds: the brotherhoods and the Church. „Though I am no admirer of our old saloons, I cannot deny that they were the poor man's club, where worker and artisan met after the day's labor to enjoy themselves among their peers" (Chr. Nielsen, 90 Years in the Danish Settlement in Chicago.")

better work than an older, but less-skilled colleague. The term "journeyman" is unknown simply because the Americans do not have apprenticeships like Europeans do. A young man starts work in a shop where he helps the other workers, and one day there is a vacancy which he fills. If he does not have the skill or if he does not learn quickly, he is dismissed and has to try his hand at another trade. Work samples or proof of knowledge are never asked of him. In this respect, and in many others, there is an unstructured and informal relationship between worker and boss. Similarly the relationship is impersonal and without any kind of consideration for each other. If there is no work for a day or two, the worker is laid off, which means he is dismissed immediately. If a worker is taken ill and a better substitute is found, the convalescent is not rehired when he reappears. As in many other cases the American displays a sublime contempt for seniority.

The days on which the artisan looks for work are discouraging. Distances between the workshops are great, and when he eventually finds a place where there is a vacancy, he may wait for hours among hundreds of applicants and then learn that every vacancy has already been filled. In this moment one understands that a worker with a family may be on the verge of dispair in this huge, merciless society ..."

Time for a celebration? Immigrant construction workers.

The American trade unions were never as politically involved as their European counterparts. Cavling explains this in the following way:

"As long as the American worker is within the walls of the factory, he is only a cog in a wheel. Europe has no idea of the discipline within these workshops. The worker not only works with his machine, he is part of it. He does not think nor does he speak. If he does not perform like a good tool, he is thrown out without sentimentality.

The worker tolerates these conditions without complaint. The machine keeps him on his toes, and his understanding of the industrial organization tells him that as long as he is there, he belongs to his boss. This daily feeling of being a mere tool, however, created the attitudes necessary for the formation of trade unions. The totally ruthless exploitation from above caused the rigid regimentation of the workers. They are armed to the teeth when they put forth their demands. And when they fight, they fight like desperate men knowing that defeat means total ruin.

General social-democratic ideas have never been in fashion in the workers' unions. Social-democrat immigrants who turn up in America with idealistic dreams of a "land of freedom" will rapidly have their eyes opened. There is no time in America for the preaching of the socialist theory. The American worker even finds the word ominous. It is generally believed that socialism is a European phenomenon which would be most unfortunate to have transplanted to American soil. This belief is so strong that the term socialist is considered abusive language among workers."

Like so many of their fellow partisans, the Danish socialists had to realize that the times were not favorable for socialism in the U.S. The founder of the Danish Social-Democratic Party, Louis Pio, emigrated in 1877 after some disagreement with the party.

One who made it!
Among the creators of the New York skyline was the son of a farmhand from Horsens, Niels Poulsen. 21 years old, he emigrated to New York as a skilled bricklayer. The pace and method, however, were unlike those in Denmark, and young Niels was reduced to a simple laborer. He quickly got the hang of the American way of building, and then things rose, in more ways than one. He started an elevator factory and participated in the erection of the New York highrises – projects which yielded fame, esteem and money. He built himself a rather spectacular house on Long Island; it was made entirely of iron and copper.

The conservative Danish government helped him, and he planned to found a model socialist settlement in Kansas. After a few months the plans had to be cancelled, and Pio settled down as a real estate dealer in Chicago. Shortly before his death in 1894, Pio established a settlement, White City, in Florida, but without the ideals that were to have formed the foundation for the Kansas settlement. The socialistic Utopia was not to be established at this time. Neither did the British socialist-utopianist, Robert Owen, nor the Norwegian composer, Ole Bull, succeed in creating their ideal communities in New Harmony, Indiana, and Oleana, Pennsylvania.

Life in the Cities

Compared to those in Denmark, wages in the U.S. were good, despite the hard work. Real wages were definitely higher. Although the cost of living (i.e. food prices and particularly rent) was higher than in Denmark, the higher wages enabled Americans to save money, so that after a couple of years they were able to buy their own homes.

A newly-arrived immigrant settled down among his fellow countrymen. In Chicago the area around Milwaukee Avenue gradually became a Danish community with Danish shops and a wide range of Danish associations. Later many Danes preferred the area around Humboldt Park, and the old Danish neighborhood was taken over by Italians and Poles. Around 1900 about 4,000 Danes lived in the Humboldt Park district. They were mainly well-to-do-workers, almost all of whom owned their own houses. All the property along prosperous Dania Avenue belonged to two rich Danish immigrants.

"... The impression you get of this avenue is one of general wealth. On every other house there is a sign written in Danish which bears an old Copenhagen name ..."

In 1893 Louis Pio, the tall, thin man wearing a hat, tried to establish a Danish settlement in White City, Florida, some 100 miles north of Miami. The operations involved, however, broke down his impaired health, and in June 1894 he died after having been ill for a short time. The settlement continued, though on a much smaller scale than its founder had imagined.

HELL'S KITCHEN.

The Story of Jacob A. Riis is the portrait of an extraordinary Danish immigrant, a Danish dreamer's meeting with the American reality and the realization of the American Dream.

"... one half of the world does not know how the other half lives. Somebody has to present the facts. That's why I became a reporter.."

"... my whole life is influenced by my long acquaintance with Jacob Riis whom i am tempted to call the best American I ever knew ..."

Teddy Roosevelt,
President of the U.S.
(1901-1909)

Society's Conscience

Jacob Riis' most impacting and enduring contribution to America and to the writing of American history lies in the hundreds of articles, lectures and books he wrote dealing with "how the other half lives." He describes the conditions among the wretched of the earth, particularly in the big cities, and those who paid the price for the wealth of others.

His subjects were the many losers who helped create the winners, and the idea of success which formed the core of the American Dream.

Riis worked for the thousands of people who were forced to live under conditions which were grotesque distortions of the notion of America as God's country and where each individual was the master of his own destiny. This "half" of America was not the same land "where roasted geese flew onto the tables," where money grew on trees and where the opportunity for happiness, wealth, freedom and success was eternally present.

Daylight changed the American Dream into a terrifying nightmare in the slums of the big cities, particularly in New York and in Chicago, which were the two main focuses of Riis' work. In many ways his analyses and reports equal the works performed by Frederich Engels in London and Wilhelm Reich in Germany. It was revealing, searching and well-documented journalism which not only presented a theory, but also a sharp remedial strategy.

Riis attained a special status in that he was the first journalist to use photography to substantiate the conditions he described.

"... a drawing would not have provided the kind of proof I wanted ... I wrote and wrote without producing any of the necessary results."

But then he began using photography, and here he was helped by a German invention: the *blitz*. It was more or less a flashlight which enabled him to take pictures in even the darkest of corners. With the help of friends and associates, he began his nightly picture rounds to disclose the inhuman conditions under which "the other half lived, carefully to let the light in where it was so badly needed."

All his actions were of substance, not theory. They always involved a human life-story, frequently a tragedy. This was his strong point. Yet when seen in a proper political perspective, it was probably his weakness also, since he did not always grasp the true facts of the case.

Jacob A. Riis (1845-1914).

The Power of Facts – and the Confusion

He was not affiliated with any specific political party or ideology. He saw himself as the free, independent reporter who was able to criticize social conditions by presenting "the facts". He clearly held in contempt all political professionals and the systems which they exploited. He supported individual politicians, but only in certain specific cases. His closest ally through the years was Theodore Roosevelt, "America's Teddy Bear". He felt he could use the politician, but in reality he was the one who was exploited. He did achieve great results such as the clearing out of slums, the establishment of some social institutions, and an awareness of ecological issues in the legislature, among others. But were they anything but superficial improvements? A kind of "social make-up" to veil the need for a fundamental and sweeping change in social conditions?

There are many interesting parallels between him and the Danish politician, Peter Sabroe, regarding work, style and attitude. They differed, however, in one essential point: Sabroe was deeply-rooted in a political party, the Social Democratic Party, which he used fully for any purpose. Riis was guided by an idealism which bordered on a naiveté, a simple-mindedness, a Christian humanism which was his strength. But he lacked the confirmation of being rooted in an established political theory. This might explain the surprising shift in his life – from sharp social criticism to almost ultra-conservative attacks against those he fought for. He found himself in a complex dilemma: on the one hand he felt total solidarity with the oppressed, the victims of slumlords and a liberalistic system; on the other hand he was a critical opponent of many of these victims because he did not fully grasp the reasons for their predicament. Or rather, he was unable to keep track of rapid development in an industrial society.

"Give the workers an opportunity to earn so much that they can live reasonably. Do not turn them into paupers by giving them alms which ori-

Reporter office at 301 Mulberry Street.

ginate in fortunes that have been accumulated through their work. In former times it was of the utmost importance to acknowledge the existence of dangerous classes in New York ..., but the danger lies not in their offences and crimes, but in the criminal ignorance of the members of the other classes. The social danger does not come from those who live in poverty and slums. It comes from a class whose fortunes have been accumulated through usury, scandalously low wages and ill-spent wealth – the class from which such atrocities are only to be expected.''

It is a wonder that he did not become a revolutionary: an anarchist, a socialist or a social-democrat. On the contrary, he kept his distance from the critical left-wingers, although in reality he was their spokesman. He ended by disowning the political radicals and he openly attacked those who abused social benefits. This demonstrates the divided consciousness which guided his work and drove him toward the sort of free-floating humanism which was his true conviction.

''All support which encourages a parasitic life, all philanthropy which stifles ambition and prevents individual efforts is despicable, even criminal. An attitude which may be healthy in an ideal society is non-progressive in a liberal, competitive society because each single individual's will and ambition is subject to the laws of the class-ridden society and the free economy.''

These contrasts made Riis so provocative and so very controversial, especially in Denmark and America with their high social ideals and their cut-throat realities.

No matter what position Jacob A. Riis attained in the U.S., he expressed quite well the culture-clash, even culture-shock which so many immigrants experienced when they contrasted America's opportunities with their homelands' limitations.

Telling the story about ''those underneath'' became his life. He waged a long battle to improve conditions among the poorest in the slums, and struggled to let the sun shine into the darkest corners.

He emigrated because of his lust for adventure, his need to seek out the great opportunities and because of an unhappy love.

Good fortune finally came his way. He happened to meet a former teacher. This led to a job with the New York News Association and thus began his career as a police reporter.

He soon did well and became an important, well-respected man in America, and eventually he married his Elizabeth.

For years prior to that, he had experienced one ordeal after another. After arriving in 1870, Riis worked at all sorts of jobs, such as in an iron-works, a shipyard, as a farmhand, and as a laborer in the forests and in the mines.

He also tried his hand at trapping, carpentry, laying rails and giving lectures, just as he also tried to sell furniture, irons and books. He scraped through without any help from the Danes to whom he might have turned. These three to four years were probably the most important in his life because he got to know society at the bottom. He tried the life of those he later wrote about, but he did not want to become one of them. He worked his way up by sheer will-power. ''I came with one pair of strong hands and with an obstinacy for two.''

It is this duality which makes his work so intriguing.

The Life of Jacob A. Riis

Jacob A. Riis (1849-1914) was the third child in a family of fifteen, including an adopted niece. His father, a grammar school teacher in Ribe, had high hopes for his children, though none of them was able to meet any of his expectations. With his extraordinary career Jacob was the one who came closest to realizing his father's dreams. He was trained as a carpenter, but made a name for himself as a reporter and social reformer in America. The most important works among his hundreds of articles, essays and books are bound in a single volume entitled ''How the Other Half Lives'' (1890), and his excellent autobiography, ''The Making of an American'' (1901).

''... One half of the world does not know how the other half lives, nor does it care. The half that is on top cares little about the struggles and even less about the destiny of those underneath, as long as it is able to hold them down and keep its own seat. (Riis, 1890)''

When he became a police reporter in New York, he met Teddy Roosevelt, who was then police commissioner. This was the beginning of a life-long, close friendship and co-operation. Their battle against slums and poverty yielded results, although many of the radicals thought that the price was too high, and that the wrong people were paying the price. They also found that the efforts to clear the slums and the other reforms were far from sufficient.

Jacob Riis was the untiring mole working behind the scenes of municipal and national comittees. At the same time he travelled extensively to lecture and show his photographs of the dismal slums and their spectacular alternatives: parks and large, airy apartment buildings with clean water and other improvements in sanitary conditions.

Several recreational areas have been named after him. The vast public beach which can be seen when flying into J.F.K. Airport in New York is called Jacob A. Riis Beach as a beautiful symbol of his battle for "light, clean air and clear water", although succeeding generations have not maintained it in quite the same spirit.

A „scrub" with her bed.

The Photograph as Documentation

About the many young criminals:
"They were not thieves by heredity; circumstances made them so. They are being created every day, and the streets and jails are the factories."

"It seemed to me that the reporter's trade was the highest and most distinguished of all; nobody else was able to tell right from wrong and to fight injustice in the world."

Riis became an excellent reporter and he was the first reporter to show the power of the photograph as a journalistic weapon. His results were unique, and the effect of the pictures exceeded his expectations. However, he saw himself as a mediocre photographer:

"I am sorry to have to say here that I was far from good as a photographer, because that was what I would have wanted to be."

Posterity does not agree with him. During the last decade a new wave of young photographers honored Riis not only as a reporter but also as a photographic artist.

A Russian immigrant and photographer, Alexander Allandt, invented an exceptional method of preservation, so that today Jacob Riis' original pictures are preserved and can be seen in the New York City Museum.

BURGLAR AT 18

HIGHWAYMAN AT 18

BURGLAR AT 17

HIGHWAYMAN AT 17

HIGHWAYMAN AT 18

PICKPOCKET AT 13

MURDERER AT 19

PICKPOCKET AT 15

HANGED AT THE TOMBS

On the Battle to Clear out the Slums:
Conditions were inhuman; „You have no more right to kill people with poor housing than with axes," Riis wrote about the capitalists and the politicians.

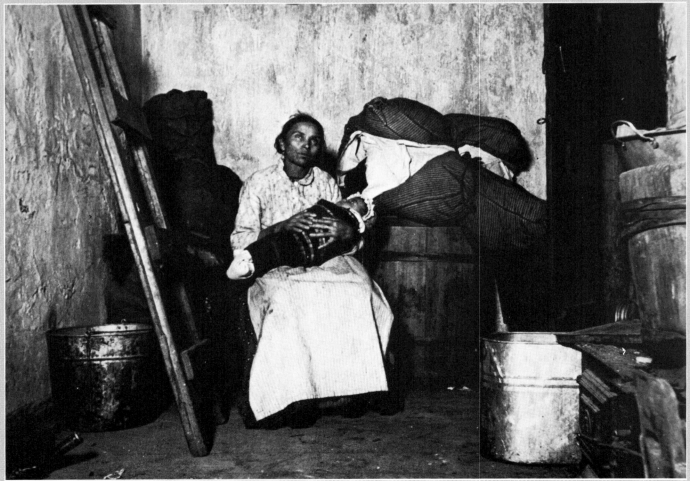

„Even the lousiest tenements were sheer luxury compared to the conditions of the people in the streets. They were thrown at the mercy of boarding-houses, dives or, as here, a police lodging-house."

„When I look upon that unhappy girl's face I am convinced that the grace of God can reach this lost woman in her sins; but what about the man who made a profit on the slum that gave her up to the streets?"

„Waifs, a common sight, were anonymous tragedies. Even in death the poor have no name.
In the common trench of the Poor Burial Ground they lie packed three stories deep, shoulder to shoulder, crowded in death as they were in life, to save space.
For even on that barren island the ground is not for the exclusive possession of those who cannot afford to pay for it."

The battle for better housing and orphanages, clean water and other sanitary improvements was a battle against political corruption and despots, but it yielded results. Copious clearings „let the light in" and gave room for public play-grounds and parks.

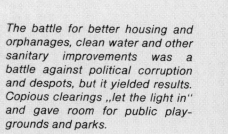

„.... it is one of the most touching sights in the world to see a score of babies, rescued from homes of brutality and desolation, ... too often their white night-gowns hide tortured little bodies and limbs cruelly bruised by human hand. To many, the Foundling Asylums became a new start in life, and the parks brought a silver lining to an otherwise black slum."

DIVIDED HEARTS.

Like all the other ethnic groups in America there were some Danes who wanted to preserve their national heritage, traditions and customs. The question of whether the Danish cultural heritage should be kept alive, or whether assimilation into the surrounding society should be sought by abandoning old-world customs, created a strong tension among the Danish-Americans. This cultural disagreement is clearly reflected in the history of the Danish Church in the U.S.

There were many reasons why "Danishness" was subjected to pressure abroad. Above all, Danish traditions were rooted in a different intellectual fellowship under other material conditions in another society. The connection between work, intellectual pursuits, religion and church festivals was changed in the new, more difficult life-situations. Competition was much more intense, and the settlers expended most of their strength trying to be active members of the new society. The work was new; the methods and tools were different. Even the traditional Danish co-operatives attained new dimensions. This limited the display of Danishness to high schools and churches, an isolation which made it difficult to define it.

On top of this came the numerous religious creeds and factions which brought internal conflicts across the ocean to America. Here the faiths were defended with a fanatic dogmatism, totally out of proportion with the importance of church and high schools in society: In 1910 only 20 % of all Danish-born Americans were members of the Danish religious community. But clergymen were not idle as to literary production; therefore their debates dominate the Danish-American source material. In contrast, the radical political movements with their social-democratic visions were hardly discernible in these debates. This is surprising considering how widespread and important they were.

The Danish Church in America

As stated above, the development of the Danish Church in America clearly reflected the principal debate concerning the preservation or the abandonment of the Danish cultural heritage. Around 1870 the Danish Church began to organize its work for the immigrants. The Society for the Promotion of the Preaching of the Gospels among Danes in America was formed, and in 1871 a vanguard of three men was sent out: a pastor, a lay preacher and a missionary student. They were to track down the places where the Danes had settled and evaluate the need for Danish clergymen. The need was great apparently, and the vanguard sent home the following unambiguous message: "Send more pastors, there is plenty of room for them." Thus several lay preachers and teachers found a vocation in America. They went through a brief education in Askov Folk High School, and were then sent off to the new country supported by the Society.

At that time most Danish settlers lived under very difficult conditions. Amidst all the strange surroundings the community and its church came to symbolize something familiar as well as a new community and a new hope. The building of small churches on the prairie was often the first visible sign that a group had settled down permanently. In a Danish-American novel a farmer explains why so much labor and money went into the church and the vicarage: "Nobody made us build them; they were not established through taxes or duties. Since we were here on the prairie, we collected the money not from our surplus, but from our poverty – simply because we needed it."

In the beginning of the 1870s the number of Danish communities rose considerably, and about 50 new congregations were founded. The first pastors were generally as poor as the settlers themselves. Their wages depended on contributions from the members of the congregation, and many of them had to resort to farming. A great part of their work consisted of a kind of visiting mission, that is in serving small enclaves that were unable to support a church and clergyman. During the first years the pastors served very large congregations. Thus one pastor's parish was the entire state of Iowa, while another served all of Kansas.

In 1870 an evangelical association was founded called "The Danish Church in America". As far as creed and other religious matters the members viewed themselves as an integral part of the established Church in Denmark, just as there was a close connection to other religious trends in Denmark. Gradually they became more and more conscious of the growing conflict between the Grundtvigians and the Inner Mission.

The Grundtvigians discussed the connection between religion and people's lives. This contrasted sharply with the Inner Mission which maintained that there was only one essential need in life: to be saved by faith in God. After the transference of the two perspectives to America, the conflict grew. Its essence became a matter of preserving or abandoning "Danishness".

Schools and Folk High Schools

The first Danish school was established in 1873, and in the 1870s and 80s more and more schools were founded in the small Danish towns throughout the Midwest. The expenses for the teachers and the buildings were often so great that many towns only organized Saturday and Sunday schools. Besides, during the summer vacation of the other American schools, Danish-American schools were still in session. The children had to learn the Danish language, Danish history and geography, and to appreciate the Danish traditions as the Grundtvigians knew them.

To many people, particularly the pastors, it was important that the young Danes in America be educated in folk high schools. Many of the immigrants had attended folk high schools in Denmark, and the majority of the clergymen were educated at Askov Folk High School during the 1870s and 80s. They thus had educational precedence, and when the folk high schools were established towards the end of the 1870s, they were more or less identical to their precursors in Denmark.

The education was based on lectures about subjects within Danish history and literature. Gradually English became a major subject. The first Danish-American folk high school was erected in the large Danish settlement in Elk Horn, Iowa, in 1878, and the next was built in Ashland, Michigan, in 1882. In Nysted, Nebraska, and Danebod, Minnesota, schools were established in 1887 and 1888, respectively. Atterdag High School in Solvang, California was founded in 1914, and the last school was established in Dalum, Canada, in 1921.

One of the most prominent men within the folk high school movement, Kristian Østergaard, held the following viewpoint: "We transported the Danish folk high school to America, but for many years America remained a foreign continent to us. In our minds and in our hearts we lived in Denmark and with all that was Danish. Of the American intellectual life we knew nothing."

Two of the Danish folk high schools in America: Ashland and Danebod in Tyler, Minnesota. Both schools had pupils well into this century. Today Danebod holds short-term courses where Danish and American culture is discussed.

A "New Denmark"?

In 1883 a Danish immigrant described his view of the future "New Denmark": "... The day may come when the English language will be totally superfluous to us. What would prevent the Danes here from settling down and cultivating territories where they had their own schools, churches and judges, so that they could fully lead their own lives. I do not think the government would object because here there is freedom for anyone who will submit to the law. In this way we Danes might establish a free state within the free state ..."

The idea of gathering together the Danes scattered throughout the various settlements was immediately seized upon by teachers and pastors, as well as farmers. The Danish Church bought a large tract of land in Minnesota in 1884, and within a few years the Tyler settlement grew into an efficiently working society with several hundred inhabitants, a Danish school and folk high school, cooperative undertakings and several communities. From 1884 to 1931 ten Grundtvigian settlements were established from southern Texas to Canada. Names like Dannevang, Askov, Dagmar, Solvang, Dalum and many more grew gradually into small Danish towns. In all of them the religious community formed the core. These were the Grundtvigian strongholds which for many years survived as "Danish" dots on the map of America.

The Happy Danes and the Holy Danes

The Inner Mission faction within the Danish Church took a long time to make itself known to the public. As mentioned above the pastors considered one thing as "essential", and they cared for their flocks in silence. They saw dealing with the historical and cultural background as a deviation from the real purpose of the Church. They particularly objected to the establishing of the Grundtvigian association, Dansk Folkesamfund (Danish Folk Community), in 1887. This association was to function as a popular, religious counterpart to the increasing number of Danish associations in the cities such as the Danish Brotherhood and Dania.

The pastors who were faithful to their Bible were fed up. One of them wrote: "Now the Danish pastors are tired of preaching God's Word to the people. Now they want to create a popular Denmark with games and songs. Preaching salvation to compatriots will then have to wait till after death."

Gradually the schism between the two factions grew. Personal conflicts between the leaders contributed to the growing intransigence, and pretty soon even the most minute item could create a dispute. The disagreements concerning the management of the Danish liturgical school

Dansk Luthersk Kirke, Askov, Minn.

Dalum, Canada.

in West Denmark, Wisconsin, raised their ire. The annual conventions grew increasingly heated, and in 1894 a final breach was caused when the Inner Mission faction decided to march out. At this time the church had around 160 congregations, a similar number of chairs (smaller communities) and close to one hundred pastors. Many congregations were divided. In several instances there were even legal battles concerning the right to church building and properties. The majority of the congregations followed the Inner Mission and only a small number of pastors remained with the Danish Church.

The United Church: Missionizing above All

A few years after the breach the Inner Mission faction united with a small fundamentalist Danish community which until that time had functioned as a branch of a Norwegian community. Thus the United Church was formed. This Church was run according to the guidelines formulated in the Danish Inner Mission. Lay preachers were sent out to new settlements to do missionary work. More pastors joined in and meetings were held with fervent preaching and singing.

This purposeful missionizing rapidly yielded results, and soon the United Church became not only the largest Danish religious community, but the largest Danish organization as well. In connection with their liturgical college in Blair, Nebraska, Dana College was founded as an institution of higher learning for young Danes. The United Church was connected to Danish immigrants in many ways. Towards the turn of the century the increasing interest in land in the northern states and on the Canadian prairie made the

Carneval in Askov, Minnesota. Askov was one of the most successful Grundtvigian settlements. They built their own co-operative institutions; they also observed traditions and festivals, where people celebrated their mutual cultural background.

Church take an active part in securing home-steads for Danish farmers while it was still possible. Half a dozen church settlements were founded in this manner.

In many ways the United Church found it easy to adjust to socio-economic development. Children born in America of Danish parents were not inclined to speak Danish, nor to preserve a Danishness far removed from them. This large group held the future, and the United Church fully knew and understood this.

They decided to switch to English because the majority of the community used this language. After all, language was just a means to reach people.

The Gospel was the ultimate authority. In the 1920s English was used more frequently at services and meetings. By changing to this lan-guage immigrants other than Danes might be reached. Thus the United Church gradually became an American institution. In 1960 they joined other churches in forming "The American Lutheran Church".

The Die-hard Danishness

During the years following the breach in 1894 the Danish Church, which continued as a Grundtvigian community, had some problems adjusting to the changing conditions. Fewer Danish schools were maintained, and the English language became the common language for most people. After the turn of the century the dream of a little Denmark in America began to fade. The folk high schools were still functioning, and a real college was established at Grand View, Iowa, in 1896.

More settlements were founded, but now iso-

Students at Dana College, Blair, Nebraska. Today Dana College offers courses of greatest interest to Danish-Americans, such as Danish language and literature.

lation from the surrounding society seemed to be a distinct aim. Security was sought and found in the small local Danish communities, thus offering protection against the unpleasant development surrounding them. In the long run the Grundtvigian communities were forced to adopt the English language. This did not happen without many heated discussions, and not until the end of the 1930s did English come to prevail in the communities. Some settlements used Danish exclusively as late as the 1940s, and many families did so even longer. The Danish Church ceased to exist as an independent association in 1962 when it joined other Scandinavian associations in "The Lutheran Church in America".

Even today the vestiges of Grundtvigian tradition are present in some of the small settlements, such as an association which publishes a magazine with a Danish Church section. The Grundtvigian influence is still felt in the cultural and religious life of the descendants of Danish immigrants.

N.F.S. Grundtvig (1783-1872)

Towards the end of his life and even more so after his death, N.F.S. Grundtvig was a key figure in Danish cultural heritage as an inaugurator and a land-mark reconciler. Through his person the spiritual revivals among the farmers were integrated back into the Established Church, and the foundation for a people's church in a democratic society was created. Through him Christianity combined with the democratic-populist movement of that time: the farmers' co-operative movement.

In his early years as the avant-garde of the first generation of romantic poets he translated Danish history which otherwise had been left on a shelf and forgotten. And later he composed numerous hymns and songs for use in churches, schools, assembly halls and houses, which since then have maintained their popularity in Denmark.

His most ardent followers called themselves "Grundtvigians", (he himself always kept aloof from that label). They dominated the church, the cultural associations, not to mention the schools in the latter half of the 19th century. His vision of a free high school for the people, based on "the living word" instead of Latin and exams was realized and spread rapidly. His light and open brand of Christianity formed the firmest of foundations for the new Danish church.

In January 1851 his wife, Lise, died and he was left a widower with three children. He then married Marie Toft towards the end of that year. Theirs was a strong, happy, but brief marriage. In the spring of 1854 Marie gave birth to a son, who was christened Frederik Lange Grundtvig. When Frederik was two months old Marie Toft died and Grundtvig was widowed again, but this time with an infant. By this time he himself was 70 years old. Four years later he married Asta Reedtz. By then he was a living monument, the closest the

N.F.S. Grundtvig.

Danish religious community ever has come to a patriarch, when his son was born. In 1860 Asta gave birth to a daughter. In 1861 he was appointed bishop of Sjaelland amid massive celebrations.

"First human, then Christian: thus are the ways of life." These were his words and he lived by them.

When the Danish defeat in the war with Germany (1864) shattered the hopes of a future for Danish democracy, Grundtvig protested so violently and behaved so irregularly that he was suspended from his job and labelled insane. This was all later forgotten, however, and it did little to harm his popularity. It did underline the fact that none of his aspects as clergyman, poet, teacher or politician had priority. He was all these rolled into one, but above all else he was a human being with violent emotions. For this reason he had been the central figure during the first years of Danish democracy.

Frederik Lange Grundtvig

Frederik Lange Grundtvig (1854-1903) was an 18-year-old student when his father died. After nine restless years of sporadic study, he graduated in social science. In the summer of 1881 he married Kristina, a farmer's daughter from Sweden, and four days after the wedding the newly-wed couple boarded a ship to cross the Atlantic and settle in the U.S.

The first great wave of immigrants was well-advanced in 1881. Four years later it peaked when Estrup (Danish Prime Minister 1875-94) set up his authoritarian regime, but at that time the battle between the estate owners and the liberal farmers was in full swing, and the gap between rich and poor widened every year in Denmark. Neither social nor political reasons made Frederik Lange Grundtvig and his wife emigrate. They left to seek their own identity in the new world. Their first home was in Shiocton, Wisconsin. Here the academic Frederik Lange Grundtvig began his ornitological studies. Then he got to know Pastor Th. Helweg from the Danish church, who convinced him that his calling was a position within the Danish church somewhere in the U.S.

In 1883 Frederik Lange Grundtvig was appointed to the church in Clinton, Iowa, and from there he came to oversee the entire Danish community in the U.S., which consisted of about 100 congregations at that time.

His goal was to gather all the Danish settlements around a common creed. The basis for this was to be his father's liberal Christianity and outlook on life in general; he gathered clergymen and teachers with similar ideas around him. He was the instigator behind the establishment of Danish schools and folk high schools and he wrote a song book. He frequently wrote articles for the Danish press.

But he had his opponents, among these the Inner Mission. This faction had been formed as a branch of the Grundtvigian church in 1861, but had changed its course in 1881 under the auspices of Wilhelm Beck. Their sharp criticism of the Grundtvigians' secular open-mindedness soon reached across the Atlantic. Here it violently opposed Grundtvig's teachings and interpretations.

The biggest obstacle, however, was the subtle yet steady Americanization of Danish thoughts, customs and traditions. Frederik Lange Grundtvig belonged to the most radical wing of the church who believed that "Danishness" should only be preserved in its entirety whereas the opposite group thought that this would lead to self-ish ethnocentricity and isolation from the rest of American society.

In 1887 he founded a Grundtvig society "Dansk Folkesamfund" as a support for his line, and this led to a schism of the Danish Church in 1894. Frederik Lange Grundtvig saw this as a personal defeat. Six years later he gave up and went back to Denmark.

Before he died he saw the Liberals defeat the large land-owners and democracy re-established in Denmark. He had, however, lived and fought for another kind of "Danishness".

Frederik Lange Grundtvig and family.

Esmay Photographer. SABULA, IOWA.

DANISH-AMERICAN ART.

Two Life-stories

"To a man with skill and energy America is still the land of the future; whether the same holds true for an artist of similar talent we do not know – but why not? A country worse than ours can hardly be found these days."

(Morgenbladet, September 5, 1886 on the departure of Carl Rohl-Smith.)

During the great immigration period opinions about America differed widely, and the ideas were based on a mixture of fact, rumor and fantasy. A predominant notion among Europe's culturel elite was that America was barbaric with regard to art. In 1889 Knut Hamsun (then Knud Pedersen) published his book "Fra det moderne Americas Aandsliv", which is characteristic of this attitude. The title is rather ironic in that Hamsun thought that amid her pursuit of material goods, America had failed to develop a culture.

An early version of the American National Symbol. The artist was a Dane: Christian Gullager, 1759-1826.

This view, however, was overshadowed by the concept of America as the land of opportunity as is seen in the quotation above.

In the wake of the 300,000 Danes who had crossed the Atlantic, more than one hundred artists followed. Two of these serve as examples of the very different circumstances which artists encountered in America.

C.C.A. Christensen (1831-1912) was the oldest, but *Carl Rohl-Smith* (1848-1900) was the one to first make himself known to the public. The latter was already celebrated as one of the most talented sculptors from the Royal Academy of Fine Arts, but he was not satisfied with the challenge of casting zink figures for the cornice of *Marmorkirken* (although he did produce four figures for it). Consequently he departed for America in 1886, a move generally favored by the press.

Rohl-Smith put in fourteen years of work in his new country before he died. During this fairly brief time-span he succeeded in establishing himself as an artist and produced several big monuments including a statue of Benjamin Franklin for the 1893 World's Columbian Exposition in Chicago, and a memorial for Iowa soldiers who had fallen during the Civil War. In one instance he was called America's leading sculptor. He died, however, amid heated debate over his work on a memorial to General W.T. Sherman to be erected in Washington D.C. (Other artists wound up completing it.) In fact, controversy followed Rohl-Smith wherever he went. In Iowa they

"Mother Iowa". The Iowa Sailors and Soldiers Monument. Rohl-Smith 1894.

did not care for his figure of a nude woman. In Washington American sculptors considered him a poor artist and felt that a national monument should be the work of a native artist and not some stray European.

Others did not doubt that Rohl-Smith was *the* man for the job. He knew how to instill a likeness in his portraits, a qualification that the man in the street could appreciate.

The artist once sculpted a profile of Mark Twain, who commented favorably on the portrait, declaring that it was "exact to the life." And in 1890 when Rohl-Smith held an exhibition in Louisville, Kentucky, it was considered the greatest of compliments when a near-sighted man started talking to a bust, thinking it was the model himself.

These statements made Henrik Cavling, a re-

porter for "Politiken", fume with rage. "A Danish artist cannot imagine the hardship that being an artist in foreign land entails. Most of the decisions concerning art are made by the populace." (Fra Amerika, 1897)

The kind of statues that Rohl-Smith worked on are virtually indestructible and can still be seen in parks and plazas, but they are rarely noticed, let alone appreciated. Rohl-Smith suffered the humilation of being famous first, only to be forgotten later.

The case of Carl Christian Anton Christensen is the exact opposite. For many years he was only known among small circles, but about 60 years after his death he became famous. In 1970 he was declared "the find of the year" in American Art, and his works were labelled "American popular art".

Mount Rushmore National Memorial, South Dakota. The artist was a Dane: Gutzon Borglum, 1867-1941.

Like Rohl-Smith, Christensen had attended the Royal Academy of Fine Arts in Copenhagen through a period of 6 years (1847-1853). He never gained admission to the Academy's School of Modelling where he might have learned to draw the human body, and therefore his figures resemble the stick figures of "primitive" painters. While he was at the Academy, he was also apprenticed to a cabinet-maker. In 1850 an important event changed his life: he became a Mormon. He then set out for America with a group of other new converts, and pulled hand-drawn carts for more than 1000 miles across the prairie from Iowa City to Salt Lake City. Since 1847 this city near the Great Salt Lake in Utah had grown and become a haven for Mormons.

Christensen depicts this long and strenuous journey in several oilpaintings, and elements from it are found in his most famous work, "The Mormon Panorama". He worked on it during the years 1877-1893 and when finished, it consisted of 23 canvasses, each measuring 175 cm × 200 cm. Only 22 of them have been preserved. The individual canvasses were sown together and were meant to be shown scene by scene as a kind of film strip. They depict the history of the early Mormon Church, from the first visions of Joseph Smith, its founder in 1830, until his successor, Brigham Young, led his flock to their new home in Utah in 1847. The depiction underlines the suffering and the cruel persecutions culminating in Joseph Smith's martyrdom.

Christensen told the story in such a way that it resembled the Old Testament's account of the sufferings endured by the Israelites during the Exodus from Egypt to the Holy Land.

Christensen travelled with his "Panorama" over the winter months, when farming was at a lull – he was also a farmer – and in this way he raised money for his missionary tours of Europe.

He advocated the "true" faith and in an educational way related the story of the Mormons. Christensen had an absolute confidence in the importance of art in this, and he felt that he had fulfilled a mission. Therefore it did not matter much that he did not become the great artist he had hoped to be in his youth.

Both Christensen and Rohl-Smith found in their own ways a place in American society. The contemporary public recognized the greatest of talents in the latter, but the former appeals more to today's public. Perhaps this is because Christensen deals with the common man in his ups and downs and depicts events from everyday life in a precise, yet humourous way amid all the great drama. Christensen's life-work is of major importance as an historical documentary, and it stands as an excellent contribution to the understanding of life for the early immigrant.

From C.C.A. Christensen's Mormon Panorama.

The Mormons

On the sixth of April 1830 Joseph Smith, an American, published the so-called Book of Mormons, an unknown Gospel. Smith had found the text for the book on a number of golden plates, which he had discovered under a tree and which some angels had translated into American for him during a revelation. The fundamental idea was that the forefather of one of Israel's tribes had emigrated to America 600 years before Christ. He was the progenitor of the native American population. Founded on the Book of Mormons, Joseph Smith created „The Church of Jesus Christ of the Latter-Day Saints" in New York State.

The movement won a lot of support, just as it also met with great opposition, mainly because it allowed plural marriages, which aroused indignation among the Puritans on the East coast. Because of these prosecutions, the community moved further and further west; according to Joseph Smith, the Garden of Eden had been located in Missouri, and in the 1840s the Mormons went here and to Illinois.

In 1844, however, Smith was lynched during riots in Nauvoo, Illinois, and consequently his successor, Brigham Young, led the 5000 Mormons away from civilization and prosecution. In wagons they emigrated some 1600 miles across the vast empty prairie to the desert basin of the Great Salt Lake, where they erected the holy city, the Zion of the West.

Despite inhuman hardships during the exodus from February 1846 to August 1847, and despite the severe conditions in the desert Young succeeded in inspiring his followers to build a flourishing society. During the following years it thrived through a massive European influx. Two of Young's closest helpers, the Hansen brothers, were Danes. They translated the Book of Mormons into Danish and as early as 1848-49 missionaries were sent to Scandinavia. These were quickly expelled from Sweden and Norway, whereas the Danish Constitution of 1849 allowed freedom of religion to everybody, and thus the missionaries gathered here.

The Mormon mission had its greatest body of followers in Northern Jutland and around Copenhagen. As early as 1852 the first Mormon emigration was arranged, and before 1870 more than 6000 Danes had emigrated to Utah. Before 1920 the number of Danish Mormon emigrants reached 16.800; the majority got as far as Zion, although some lost their faith during the hardships: along the Mormon Trail numerous Danish settlements arose, created by apostates; Council Bluffs, Iowa is one of these settlements. The Danish Mormon emigration differs from the general emigration by its large number of women and children, 70 % against 48 % generally, and by recruiting its converts among the poorest in society. This is probably because there was a huge number of women among religious sects outside the Established Church, and to the poorest, single women with children, servants, factory girls and seamstresses, the Mormon mission was their only chance of emigrating as the mission financed their crossing.

Missionaries were sent over from Utah to preach in Denmark. A missionary reads from the Book of Mormon to a village carpenter in Jutland.
Oil painting by Chr. Dalsgaard, 1856.

DANISH-AMERICAN PRESS.

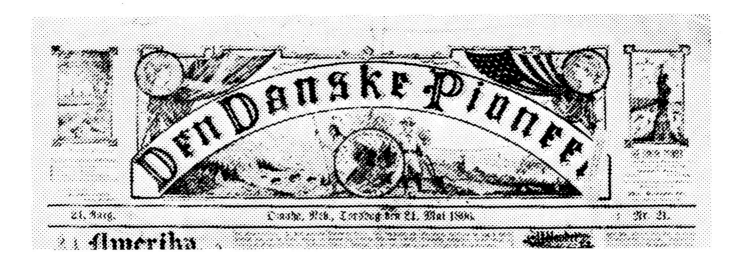

"This past week has been marked by disappointments, accidents and deaths within the settlement. On top of all this, *Den Danske Pioneer* (The Danish Pioneer) came two and a half days late" (Den Danske Pioneer, March 23, 1922).

Den Danske Pioneer was just one of the more than 200 Danish-American newspapers established by Danish immigrants. *The Pioneer* was started in Omaha, Nebraska (1872), and it turned out to be the largest and most influential of the Danish papers in America with a circulation of almost 40,000 just prior to World War I. The many subscribers anxiously awaited its delivery, often the highlight of the week. This is indicative of the isolation and loneliness endured by the vast majority of immigrants.

The Recipe for a Danish Newspaper in America

Readers submitted articles about a secluded life on the prairie, loneliness in the city, or the mere frustration at being reduced to the status of a helpless child in that English was incomprehensible to them. The Danish-American papers were thus a much-needed anchor for the many Danish immigrants during their adjustment period. At the same time the press also tempered the culture

shock among recent immigrants by preserving a connection to the homeland and the Danish language. Through the Danish-American newspapers a window was opened between two worlds. Here the Danish immigrant could find out what the American society expected from him, as well as learn what rights and opportunities he had. He could read about laws and statutes concerning his property, about his right to vote and how to acquire American citizenship. He could follow the discussions in American politics and was thus encouraged to actively participate. Danish immigrants in other (American) states provided information about living conditions and job opportunities. Advertisements informed him as to where he could buy farm equipment, medicine and clothes. He maintained connections with Denmark for as long as he felt it necessary by reading about Danish politics and the latest news from his home country. The readers were grateful for this.

"I would never have learned that my dear old aunt had died had I not seen the obituary in *The Pioneer*," wrote one immigrant from the Danish Island of Fejø (*Den Danske Pioneer,* March 23, 1922).

The newspapers were also of great importance to the many Danish-American societies which often used them to reach all their members. The papers teemed with information about meetings and celebrations. This, however, called for a delicate balancing act on the part of the editors, not only because it was time-consuming, but also because they had to be careful not to favor one society over another since this might result in the other societies cancelling their subscriptions.

Before the Turn of the Century: the Pioneer Era of the Danish-American Press

Even before *Den Danske Pioneer,* other attempts had been made to establish a Danish press in the U.S. This was done in cooperation with Norwegian immigrants in the 1850s. The Danish immigrants were still so few that an all-Danish newspaper was not feasible. Since the linguistic differences between Danish and Norwegian were easily reconciled, it was only natural that the Danish and Norwegian immigrants cooperated in publishing a Danish-Norwegian newspaper. The first of these, *Skandinavia,* was established in New York (1847). Like so many of these "pioneer" newspapers, it only lasted for a short time.

The boom of Danish immigration just prior to and throughout the 1890s gave a real impetus to the Danish-American press. Among this multitude of new-comers was Sophus Neble (1862-1931), a printer's apprentice from Stubbekøbing. He emigrated to America in 1883

During its first years „Den Danske Pioneer" was published from this house in Omaha.

to seek his fortune, and more than anybody else he became synonymous with the Danish-American press to later generations. After a brief, unsuccessful attempt at farming in Wisconsin, Sophus Neble was employed at *Den Danske Pioneer* in 1883. The founding-owner of the paper was Mark Hansen, a Civil War veteran who had tried his hand at mule-driving, carpentry, running a grocery store, and politics. Hansen, a Democrat, started his newspaper as a response to another new Danish paper in Omaha, *Nebraska Skandinav,* which was run by Republicans. Shortly thereafter Hansen managed to buy out his political opponents.

In 1887 Mark Hansen sold *Den Danske Pioneer* to Sophus Neble who maintained the paper's political persuasion. The paper was marked by socialist tendencies towards the turn of the cen-

tury. The editorials toyed with the idea of establishing a socialist party in America, and periodically the paper published articles written by Danish immigrant socialists. During the great lockout of 1899 in Denmark, more than $ 9,000 was raised from subscribers for the families who were without work during the four months of conflict.

Naturally the paper sharply critized the conservative government in Denmark which, according to *Den Danske Pioneer,* suppressed democratic rights. Various editorials encouraged the Danes to rebel and to oust King Christian IX and Prime Minister Estrup. This instigation to revolution resulted in the paper's being banned in Denmark for twelve years (1886-1898). Neble, however, succeeded in smuggling copies to the many subscribers in Denmark, either enclosed in an envelope or under another name.

Sophus Neble made The Danish Pioneer into the greatest Danish newspaper in the US. He never cared for the King, nor for Estrup, Prime Minister 1875-94, and as he attacked both in his paper The Pioneer was banned in Denmark over a period. Sophus Neble loved fishing and hunting. This depicts his office with his hunting trophies.

The Wide Range of Danish-American Newspapers

By around the turn of the century Sophus Neble had solved the financial problems of *Den Danske Pioneer* and had improved Danish-American relations. In 1903 a proud Neble accounted for the success of the paper:

"Over the last couple of years, *Den Danske Pioneer* has prospered like no other Scandinavian paper in America. There are very few Danes in America who do not read the paper ... *Den Danske Pioneer* is the friend of laborers and farmers ... *Den Danske Pioneer* stands up for the Danes in America ..." *(Den Danske Pioneer,* October 8, 1903). Other Danish-American papers tried to compete with *Den Danske Pioneer.* Thirty-four Danish and twenty-four Danish-Norwegian papers were established towards the end of the 1800s, but after the turn of the century only fifteen remained. Danish newspapers flourished in American cities with a high influx of Danes: the socialistic *Revuen* in Chicago (1895-1952), the intellectual *Nordlyset* in New York (1891-1953), and *Bien* in San Francisco (1882-   ). There were also religious papers because, in spite of all their theological conflicts, both the Grundtvigians and the Inner Mission agreed that the Danish-American papers were too secular.

The Inner Mission published *Danskeren* (1892-1921), the Grundtvigians *Dannevirke* (1880-1931). In Utah the Danish Mormons published *Bikuben* which ran for almost 60 years. The toughest competitors for *Den Danske Pio-*

neer, however, were a number of papers from Minneapolis, St. Paul, Chicago and Racine, Wisconsin, published by Christian Rasmussen. In many ways he was Sophus Neble's exact opposite. Rasmussen was a Republican while Neble, as has been stated, was a Democrat. While *Den Danske Pioneer* encouraged the Americanization of Danish immigrants, Rasmussen saw it as his main objective to preserve the Danish heritage. Above all, Rasmussen was a businessman. From his big firm in Minneapolis – known by Danish-American as "the paper factory" – he published *Ugebladet* (1881-1959), *Chicago-posten, Racine-posten* and *St. Paul-posten,* reaching a total circulation of 22,000. These papers differed from *Den Danske Pioneer* in that they contained far more advertisements. Rasmussen also published Danish books in America and ran an agency which represented seventy-five Scandinavian magazines. The Danish immigrants published not only newspapers, but almanacs, Christmas catalogs, weekly journals and books as well. *Spøgefuglen* ("The Jester", 1893-1935), a fun magazine, was very popular due to the typically Danish dry sense of humor in its articles and political satires of Danish and American events.

Another widely-read magazine, *Kvinden og Hjemmet* (1888-1948) was published in Danish-Norwegian and Swedish editions with a total circulation of 80,000. In its pages appeared such articles as knitting instructions, recipes, "do-it-yourself" hints and serialized stories taken from Scandinavian and American women's magazines.

120

Hey-day for the Danish-American Press

The period 1900-1914 was the hey-day for the Danish-American press. Immigration provided a growing number of readers and the established newspapers increased their circulation as never before. *Den Danske Pioneer* took the lead with a circulation which rose from 26,323 in 1901 to almost 40,000 in 1914. This was also, however, the period when Danish immigrants realized the increasing difficulty in maintaining a Danish-American identity. America's participation in World War I gave rise to a violent opposition against immigrants from American nationalists. Danish immigrants in Iowa were accused of being "100 % Danish" and not wanting to become Americans. The Danish-American press spoke up on behalf of the Danish immigrants during this conflict. Sophus Neble wrote profusely about the patriotic activities of the Danish-Americans during the war and protested vehemently against the accusations of un-American attitudes. Nevertheless many Danes stopped speaking Danish for fear of seeming unpatriotic. They were eager to demonstrate their loyalty to America.

Years of Crisis

The 1920s marked a turning point for the Danish-American press. In 1910 the seven biggest Danish-American papers had a total number of 72,000 subscribers. Twenty years later, in 1930, the total had fallen to 37,000. The main reasons for this were the Americanization of the second and third generations and a decline in immigration. The laws concerning immigration quotas allowed a mere 5,970 Danes to enter in 1921. Throughout the 1920s this quota was reduced even further.

Some Danish editors tried to reach second- and third-generation Danish-Americans by printing articles in English. They were anxious to preserve what little remained of the Danish heritage in America. Other editors, such as Sophus Neble, were more realistic about the future of the Danish-American press: "The foreign language press will continue in America as long as there are men and women here who speak more fluently in languages other than English ... and since this sphere is being narrowed, Den Danske Pioneer will eventually become one of the typically American papers written entirely in English. This will be an even progression. Any foolish attempt to accelerate or delay this process will inevitably fail (Den Danske Pioneer, February 16, 1922)."

Sophus Neble, usually the radical editor of The Danish Pioneer, Omaha, Nebraska, shot in his parade uniform as titular serving the Governor of Nebraska during World War 1. (no. 3 from the left).

The Danish „newspaper king", Christian Rasmussen, published several newspapers from this printing house in Minneapolis. He also edited a number of Danish novels and poems.

Survivors of a Century

Neble predicted the death of the Danish-American press within the near future, but in 1986, some 114 years after its inception in Omaha, *Den Danske Pioneer* is still being published in Chicago with a circulation of 3,000. *Bien* in Los Angeles and the Grundtvigian magazine, *Kirke og Folk,* in Des Moines, Iowa, are the only remaining Danish-American periodicals.

What Neble could not predict was the revived interest in cultural heritage experienced in American society during the 1960s and 70s. The subscribers to these publications can be divided into two groups. Some are elderly people who arrived in America during the 1920s and 30s and who are bilingual, yet want to maintain some connection with Denmark. Others are grandchildren and great-grandchildren of Danish immigrants who have taken an active interest in their Danish background, but who read and speak very little Danish.

Den Danske Pioneer has molded itself to the readership. The strong political nature of the paper under Sophus Neble has given way to friendly and serene articles from Danish settlements in the U.S. The articles bringing news from Denmark are very popular. They offer, however, a somewhat distorted picture of the old country. The readers seem to prefer articles about the royal family and the national soccer team.

There is only a slight hint of an authentic Danish identity left in the paper, but as long as *Den Danske Pioneer* and other Danish-American publications and organizations exist, they bear witness to the fact that the Danish immigrants did not disappear without a trace.

IN PURSUIT OF DREAMS.

"The Dream of America" tells the story of how Danes left their homeland and sought new lives in a new land. It has examined who these people were, where they came from, why they left and where they went. It has also suggested to a certain extent what their experience was once they arrived. This story has been retold in greater detail in the pages of this book. But in a sense the story is not complete until it has been told as a part of a much larger story, the story of many immigrants from many lands who taken together have shaped the American experience, enriching it, but also creating problems which American society has sometimes found difficult to solve. It is this larger story which has shaped the experience of the children and grandchildren of these Danish immigrants.

Assimilation or Ethnic Identity?

In many ways the story of the Danish immigrant experience is also the story of every other immigrant group that has come to America. Their stories could be told in similar exhibits. The names would be different, the artifacts might reflect different folk traditions, but the conditions and the experience would be similar for a multitude of peoples coming to the United States from countries all over the world. Each group has had to struggle with the question of a changing identity. On the one hand each group has had its own ethnic identity, a complex variation of identifying characteristics among these being national, religious, linguistic, ancestral or physical characteristics. On the other hand, most groups have had a desire to assimilate into American society and to become Americans. Some groups, like the Danes, because of their ethnic background, found it easy to assimilate. But not all groups of people shared this experience. Because of cultural, religious or racial differences, some groups were not readily welcomed by American society, and for them ethnic identity became an important unifying force in their struggle to participate fully in society.

The resulting tension between assimilation and ethnic identity has been evident throughout the two-hundred years of the American experience. At times ethnic identity has been looked upon favorably; at other times it has been viewed with suspicion. Recently in the United States, ethnic identity has become popular again. Since those Americans of Danish ancestry have never found it necessary to retain an ethnic identity, their participation in this revival of ethnic popularity has been reflected in a growing awareness and interest in ethnic heritage.

"A Teeming Nation of Nations"

The story of how the United States has been settled by peoples from many lands and by many

ethnic groups is either unknown or ignored both by Americans and peoples of other countries. America, however, is a land of immigrants, a land of diverse peoples. From the earliest tribes who wandered across the Bering Strait following game to the more recent groups coming from Vietnam or Mexico in search of work or a perception of freedom, the country is made up of immigrants. Some came out of necessity, some because they were forced, and some came out of a spirit of adventure. But no matter why they came, once they arrived they found themselves, as the American poet Walt Whitman wrote, in a ''teeming nation of nations.'' Each group brought the richness of a culture from its homeland, and each group had to somehow adapt its culture to that of the new land. Some groups, like the Scandinavians and Germans, because of ethnic background, found it easier to assimilate into what has been known as ''WASP'' culture. The word ''WASP'' comes from the first letters of the words: white, Anglo-Saxon and Protestant, and refers to those people who share these characteristics. Others, like the Irish, the Italians, the Blacks or the Chinese, because of religion or the color of their skin, had to struggle through the prejudices of the ''majority'' culture to find acceptance and prosperity.

There has been, however, no majority ethnic group. It is true that the nation owes much of its heritage to Great Britain if for nothing else than the language. But the thinking of men like John Locke and Adam Smith and their ideas of democracy and capitalism are also indelibly etched in the Declaration of Independence, the Constitution and America's economic system. It is also true that at the time of the Revolutionary War most of the population was of British background. But even before this time other groups were contributing to the richness of colonial society, the Black slaves from western Africa, the Dutch along the Hudson River, the Swedes along the Delaware River, and the Germans who settled in Pennsylvania. And elsewhere in the land that was to become the United States, the Indian, Spanish and French cultures flourished. The seeds of diversity existed before the nation was born.

The Melting Pot

The diversity continued to grow as waves of immigrants came to America's shores first primarily from northern Europe: from England, Scotland and Ireland, and from Germany and Scandi-

navia. As conditions changed and greater opportunities became available at home, emigration from these countries declined to be replaced by waves of immigrants from southern and eastern Europe, such as Italy, Greece, Russia, Poland and Czechoslovakia. By the early part of this century over a million people were coming each year to the United States. These numbers brought pressures to limit the flow, and in 1924 laws were passed setting quotas on the number of people allowed to enter the country as immigrants. In 1965 the Quota Acts were repealed and new laws enacted to control immigration. Despite these laws, upwards of a million people continue to come each year to the United States. Now, however, they come primarily from the ''Third World'', countries in south-east Asia, the Caribbean and Mexico. Their presence contributes to the diversity of the American people.

This diversity has created a problem for the American people. There is a desire for an ''American'' identity. This has led to the idea of America as the great ''melting pot'' where peoples from many nations assimilate to create a new people with freedom and equality and with a new identity. It arises out of a need to create a sense of one people with one identity out of many peoples and many identities. This view that America is a great ''melting pot'' has been the traditional view of the government and reflects the interpretation of early twentieth century historians. It has been spread by the school systems and politicians, and can be found in newspapers, and on radio and television. It finds expression in patriotic songs, patriotic organisations such as the Daughters of the American Revolution and veterans groups like the American Legion and the Veterans of Foreign Wars. This inclination reflects in part a fear of diversity and a need to create unity and a sense of nation among all the various ethnic groups which make up the American population. In times of war and economic recession, extreme feelings of patriotism have led to the persecution of fellow Americans. In the nineteenth century groups like the Irish experienced prejudice. Signs read, ''Irish need not apply,'' as they were excluded from jobs. This resulted in bitter and bloody race riots. German-Americans during World War I suffered both prejudice and violence. In some states it was even forbidden to speak German in public or in private! During World War II Japanese-Americans were held in detention centers since other Americans suspected they might aid the enemy.

Cultural Traditions and Regional Identities

While the image of the United States as the great "melting pot" is deeply felt, the experiences of each group of peoples argue against the idea of complete assimilation. What outwardly appears as an American identity is only a veneer, though an important one, covering the various cultural traditions of a multitude of peoples. These cultural traditions have been preserved, sometimes consciously but often unconsciously, and most often within the family or in a particular area where there is heavy settlement of an ethnic group. These cultural traditions have also led to various regional identities. Spanish heritage is evident in states such as Arizona, California and New Mexico. Aspects of French culture are preserved in areas of Louisiana and along the Mississippi River, and states such as Minnesota, North Dakota and Wisconsin are known for their Scandinavian population.

Various ethnic groups, despite the pressures to assimilate, have preserved cultural identity. This has occurred most often among those ethnic groups that are large enough to maintain an identity, that have experienced some kind of prejudice, or that have an interest in preserving identity because of religion. Particularly in large cities various groups have clustered to create ethnic ghettos in which are preserved language, ethnic foods and other aspects of ethnic cultures. Communities of Italians, Chinese, Poles, Japanese and others can be found in many American cities. In such communities there is a large enough population to support newspapers and social organizations which preserve ethnic cultures. Other groups such as Blacks, Chicanos (immigrants of Indian and Hispanic background from Mexico), and Native Americans have been segregated, and this has meant preservation of ethnic culture since they have been excluded from full participation in society. Finally, some groups by virtue of religion have sought to maintain an ethnic identity. This can be seen in Jewish communities or in Mennonite communities where German is spoken. In all cases, however, sufficient numbers of an ethnic group must exist to maintain a visible identity and to preserve language and social institutions.

The Ethnic Revival

In a sense the continued interest in ethnicity is a response to the very forces that would push peoples toward assimilation. Within such a large population there is a desire to have some independent identity from that of the larger population. Recent ethnic interest and pride can also be seen arising in the turbulent sixties in response to and as an outcome of the Civil Rights Movement and the war in Vietnam. Blacks during the sixties experienced a growing awareness of and a pride in themselves as a people in their struggle to achieve full equality before the law and in the eyes of society. As they found a common identity there evolved a Black pride and a realization that Blacks had a rich culture, that "Black was beautiful." This influenced the American Indians and the Chicanos. As soul music, rhythm and blues and Mexican food became popular, and as the younger generation of the sixties became aware of the spiritual visions of the American Indians, there grew a respect for these cultures which had been traditionally looked down upon.

A further contributing factor to a resurgence in ethnic interest was a feeling that the war in Vietnam was the result of the "WASP" ethic. Given the difficulty of the Vietnam experience, there was a reaction against the eastern establishment of political, industrial and intellectual leaders who were perceived as being responsible for and guiding that effort. Had the American presence in Vietnam been perceived as successful, the American people would have felt pride and a sense of national unity, but with the perceptions of defeat came an attempt to disassociate by seeking a separate identity. Interest in ethnic heritage offered a way for various groups to declare their independence from the larger society while maintaining loyalty to it.

An event which was the result of Black ethnic identity, but which in turn inspired great popular interest in ethnic heritage, was the publication of and subsequent television series based on Alex Haley's book, *Roots*. The struggle of a black man to recover his identity from the mists of history captured the imagination of many Americans who felt a similar need to find their "roots". The popular reaction to *Roots* underscores again the dilemma of the American people; there is an identity of the nation which shapes the people's public identity, but the people are also tied to independent identities of culture and heritage which are private.

The results of renewed interest in ethnic heritage can be seen in a number of ways. Perhaps the most apparent is the rise of ethnic festivals, restaurants, and a renewed interest in societies devoted to preserving culture. Tracing family genealogy has also became a popular activity. It is through these kinds of activities that most people participate in ethnicity. However, such activities tend to be superficial in nature, often celebrating an idealized remembrance of the culture through foods, folk dances and folk costumes without appreciating the role such activities played within folk culture. Nor is there often a real attempt to understand the contemporary society of the native land. Such activities, however, can create interest that may lead to more serious study of a country and culture as it existed in the past and exists today.

More serious interest in ethnicity has led to the establishment at various colleges and universities of programs devoted to the study of ethnic groups. Black, Native American and Chicano studies were established in the late sixties and early seventies, and programs devoted to various other ethnic groups enjoyed growing enrollments. Such serious study has led to a greater recognition of how different groups have participated in the history of the United States. As a result of this interest, history books have been written that pay greater attention to the ethnic and minority experience and how it helped shape the American experience, and literary anthologies have been revised to include representatives of various minority cultures. Children in the public schools are exposed to the experience of Blacks and American Indians, and they learn about such figures as Martin Luther King. Indeed, in 1986, Americans will begin celebrating Martin Luther King's birthday as a national holiday in recognition of the role he played in changing American society. Activities such as these underscore the diversity of American culture and hopefully will lead to further understanding and tolerance of this diversity.

The Danish Heritage

The resurgence of interest in Danish heritage in the United States among the children and grandchildren of Danish immigrants has mirrored the general interest in ethnicity arising in the sixties and seventies. However, since Danish immigrants seldom found it necessary to retain their ethnic identity as a matter of survival in American society, the children of these immigrants are often unaware of the rich traditions in Danish culture, the literature, music and folk arts, and only a small minority speaks the Danish language. Consequently, interest in Danish heritage has often been sentimental and commercialized. This can be seen in such places as Solvang, California, where visitors find artificial thatched roofs, half-timbered houses, bakeries, restaurants and dozens of gift shops selling items from Denmark.

Commercial activities are important in creating an interest in ethnic heritage. And yet such activities do not lead to a deeper appreciation of a people or a heritage. In an attempt to inspire serious study of the Danish immigrant heritage, and to unify interest in that experience, the Danish American Heritage Society was founded in 1977. The timing of its founding reflects again the resurgence in ethnic interest in American society. This organization has as its goal the study and publication of research into the Danish immigrant experience. Since 1977 the Danish American Heritage Society has published a journal, *The Bridge,* and it has been instrumental in laying the groundwork for the Danish Immigrant Museum to be built in Elk Horn, Iowa, the site of the first Danish Folk High School in the United States. Such a museum will provide a place where artifacts important to Danish immigration might be preserved and studied. But more importantly, it will be a place where Americans, both of Danish descent and those of other ethnic backgrounds, will be able to gain a greater understanding of the Danish experience and also an appreciation of the problems of immigration. This is a dream, but it is a dream stemming from a renewed interest by Danish-Americans in their ethnic heritage. It is a dream which has begun to take shape even in the preparation of the exhibit,"The Dream of America."

Dreams are the seeds of stories. Dreams inspired many of the immigrants who came to the United States: dreams of a better life, dreams of religious freedom, dreams of equality. For many their dreams were realized: for many others their dreams were shattered by brutal realities. The story of the United States has been the pursuit of these dreams. This too has been the story of those Danes who left Denmark to find new lives in the United States. In pursuit of their individual dreams, they have told a story, a story of struggle and hope, a story of the human experience.

THE CONSERVATION OF DREAMS.

The Nordic Heritage Museum

Nordic immigration research in America has traditionally centered on the midwestern states. The Pacific Northwest, with its considerable Nordic population, still remains a relatively unexplored area and thus should provide a fertile field for future studies. The present paper only attempts to give a quick overview of general trends while placing the Nordic Heritage Museum in its proper context in the documentation and preservation of the Nordic heritage in the Northwest.

Nordic immigration generally followed the northwesterly migration movement. From the older midwestern settlements in Illinois, Wisconsin, Iowa, Minnesota and the Dakotas the Nordics moved west settling along the Pacific coast where the mountains, forests, and rivers enabled them to assume familiar lifestyles as farmers, fishermen, lumberjacks and millworkers.

Few Nordics came to the Northwest before the Civil War or even before the 1870s, but following the completion of the Pacific Northwestern Railroad's western terminus at Tacoma in 1883 the flow of Nordics increased rapidly. They spread all over Washington, Oregon and Idaho although the largest settlements are found west of the Cascade Mountains. The growth of towns drew increasing numbers of the migrants, and urban colonies began to form, the major ones being Seattle, Tacoma and Portland. After 1890 many settlers began to arrive directly from Scandinavia, although secondary migration continued to play a very important role in the settlement of the Northwest.

Logging near Preston, Washington. 1920.

Halibut fishing.

One reason why the Northwest attracted such a large number of Nordics was undoubtedly the fact that it offered oportunities in occupations with which these immigrants were familiar. It has been documented that there is a definitive and positive relationship between occupation structure of the place of settlement and that of the place of emigration, and although Nordic Americans certainly changed their range of occupations to something that more directly reflected the general distribution among occupations in American society, there was a tendency to find work in familiar fields such as lumbering, fishing, mining, agriculture as well as in trade, construction, wood and millwork. Obviously, the region suited the Nordics very well and many immigrants spoke of their happiness at being in a place that reminded them so much of the old country, thereby making the settling-in process relatively painless.

Most of the early immigrants followed several occupations during their working years. Typical was a career that included work as a logger, a logging camp cook, a blacksmith, a shipwright and a millwright. Logging and the wood industry attracted a large number of Finns, Norwegians and Swedes throughout the region. According to one study more than 10,000 Nordics were employed in Washington's woods industry in 1900 making up 25 % of the work force. They were three times as numerous as the Japanese who ranked a number two among the national groups engaged in this industry. Mining was pursued in particular by the Finns. Important coal mining areas were found east of Seattle in Newcastle and Black Diamond. The richest mining area in the Northwest, the Coeur D'Alene Mining District, also employed, and still employs a considerable number of Nordics. In Idaho and in the eastern part of Washington, around Pullman, Colfax and

Logging near Preston. Washington. 1920.

Swedish immigrants in front of their house.

LaCross, as well as in the Willamette Valley of Oregon, Nordic settlers farmed the land and grew orchards.

The early urban settlers were often common laborers, but by the turn of the century trade and commerce increased as a source of employment. This was in part the result of the large influx of immigrant seamen who began arriving around 1900. Soon the Nordics, in particular the Norwegians, began to play dominant roles in the fishing industry. They have owned and managed packing companies, canneries, large fishing vessels and steamers and have held responsible positions in cooperatives and trade unions in the fishing industry as well as in the Association of Pacific Fisheries.

Nordic immigrant women were to a large extent housewives and domestic servants. A relatively small number held occupations as seamstresses, boarding house managers, nurses or teachers.

In many of the Nordic communities that were formed throughout the Northwest customs and traditions have remained quite strong. Lodges, churches, choirs and choruses, folkdance societies and newspapers attest to the fact that the Nordic heritage still is alive and thriving in this part of the United States.

It is the purpose of the Nordic Heritage Museum to help protect and preserve this heritage for future generations. The idea of a Nordic museum emerged many years ago but active planning did not start until 1978, when a former schoolbuilding was leased from the Seattle School Board. The building, which is located in Ballard, the center of the Nordic community in Seattle, has been extensively renovated. As far as can be determined, the Museum is the first and only museum to include all five Nordic groups in the United States.

Acquisitions in the areas of fishing, boatbuilding, farming and logging have enabled the museum to begin the buildup of what will become major permanent exhibits delineating the development of these industries in the Pacific Northwest region. Other fields of acquisitions include blacksmithing, carpentry and other city related professions. Costumes, wooden utensils, textiles as well as photographs and books are also major parts of the collection. In addition to original artifacts some archival material is being collected. The library, named for the late Professor Walter Johnson, for many years head of the Scandinavian Department at the University of Washington, is growing rapidly and contains fine examples of Nordic and Nordic-American literature.

In an effort to provide a complete educational program for the community, exhibits are supplemented by lecture and film series, concerts, plays, the Scandinavian Language Institute classes where Norwegian, Swedish, Danish, and Icelandic classes are taught, folkdancing and traditional folk art classes such as rosemaling and weaving.

Several major exhibits have come to the museum from the Nordic countries as well, including a textile exhibit from Sweden in 1982, an exhibit on Greenland which was organized by the Danish Foreign Ministry as part of Scandinavia Today, a Lapp art exhibit sponsored by the Nordic Arts Centre in Helsinki, Finland, and an exhibit of contemporary Norwegian glass, enamel and textile art. The latest effort in this international exchange is "The Dream of America" organized and sponsored by the Danish National Museum and the Prehistoric Museum Moesgaard in Aarhus, Denmark. "The Dream of America" is a superb culmination of the buildup of the Nordic Heritage Museum thus allowing this young institution to tell the whole story of the immigration to the United States and the settlement of the west.

The Danish Immigrant Museum

Danish immigration to the United States peaked in the years between 1880 and 1914. By 1980, consequently, the Danish community in the United States had seen the majority of the generation of immigrants from this flood pass away. Danish Americans were struck by their loss, as it was not only personal but also cultural and historical. Without these parents and grand parents, their own past was also lost for they had lost the stories, memories and special experiences that only these immigrants could give. In a sense the community's memory had died. What was to take its place? How was their story to be preserved? Were the last traces to disappear also?

The Danish Immigrant Museum will tell the story of people – how they came to North America, how they lived after their arrival and what they have passed on to their chilren and grandchildren. (Reunion of the Elk Horn Folk School, 1912).

Acting on this sense of urgency a committee of committed people, many already involved with Danish institutions and organizations, was formed at the suggestion of Dana College in Blair, Nebraska and the Danish American Heritage Society. This committee first explored what colleges and societies already existed to learn if they could undertake the task of saving Danish American heritage. Efforts had been made especially by clergy in the late 19th Century to preserve the bi-cultural values in younger generations. Seminaries, church related colleges such as Dana College and Grand View College in Des Moines, Iowa and folk schools had all been a part of their effort. Their efforts to preserve immigration history, however, had been limited to collecting archival and library materials. Church affiliation also meant that constituencies or audiences were often limited. The Committee soon realized that there had not been a systematic effort to preserve the material culture of the Danish immi-

grants, and their recommendation was to begin immediately a museum separate from schools, churches or fraternal organizations to preserve and interpret the artifacts and traditions of Danes in North America.

The Danish Immigrant Museum was "founded" without a collection or a location that it called home precisely because of the urgency seen by this original committee. The committee was quickly re-formed as a Board of Directors with by-laws and articles of incorporation, as a non-profit educational institution. With help from museum consultants, the Board wrote a purpose that brought into sharper focus the Museum's goals reason for being:

> The Danish Immigrant Museum will tell the story of the Danish American experience and is organized to collect, preserve, study and interpret artifacts and traditions which express the experience of Danes in America.

In 1983 Elk Horn and Kimballton, Iowa were selected as the site for the museum. Here was an area with a high concentration of Danish Americans who were anxious to work for the Museum and make it a succes. The Museum could be a "jewel," that stood out in these small towns just off a major east-west interstate highway, rather than one more cultural institution in a larger city. The enthusiasm in Elk Horn and Kimballton continued and land for the building site was donated. It is a piece of Iowa's rural landscape at its best, reminiscent of parts of Denmark with a panorama of gently rolling hills sloping away from the twenty acre site.

With the purpose as a general guide, the Board adopted a collection policy that outlined the priorities for the collection. The emphasis is on the first generation of Danes who immigrated: what they brought with them and what they made and used in North America. Since immigration continues, both historic and contemporary artifacts are accepted and sought.

To meet the needs of preservation and especially interpretation of these artifacts and traditions, howewer, the Danish Immigrant Museum looks forward to creating a contemporary museum building as its home. Working with an architect the Board and staff are sharing their dreams of programs which will make it a living museum. Demonstrations, performances and

Children have made up a large proportion of Danish emigrants to the United States. Their parents often made a conscious effort to help them appreciate their heritage as with this child in Santa Rosa, California about 1950.

outdoor festivals will help to make the past come alive.

The Danish Immigrant Museum's goal is to create a museum and building with the same warm and hospitable atmosphere of a Danish home – a place to enjoy and a place to learn, open to all. The Museum invites all to help to create this home to save Danish American heritage and to share it with others.

CANADIAN PERSPECTIVES.

Right up to World War I, the United States was by far the most attractive nation for millions of European emigrants who broke off from the old world in search of a new and better one. To most Europeans the image of Canada was then one of ice and exotic wilderness. It was believed to be a place for adventure, not settlement. Soon after the founding of the Confederation of Canada (1867), however, federal and provincial governments began to form strategies in order to attract immigrants from western Europe. Slowly but surely public agencies created a new image of Canada as the land of endless opportunity and as a garden just waiting to be cultivated.

The Dominion Land Act (1872) gave settlers the right to take up a quarter-section (160 acres) of unoccupied Dominion land for a mere $ 10 registration fee. If he cultivated his "homestead", a settler could claim ownership after three years. The law was enacted to compete with similar homestead acts in the United States. At the beginning of European mass emigration to North America, the existence of free land was no doubt the greatest attraction and a very strong motivation for leaving the old world. But for Danish emigration to Canada after World War I, it was not so important. Most of the land available for homesteading was on the periphery in more than one sense. Most Danes bought or rented in already-settled areas.

Canadian efforts to recruit new citizens were first directed towards the British Isles, but later the range of preferred immigrants was extended to all of western Europe and Scandinavia in particular. In the early 1870's, the provincial governments of New Brunswick and Manitoba were active in Denmark. A Danish party settled in Montrose, Manitoba, and in 1872, one Captain Heller led a party of 29 Danish immigrants up the St. John River in New Brunswick where a block of land had been made available for Danish settlement. Soon "Hellerup", later called "New Denmark", was established. Woodland was cleared and eventually a prosperous community based on potato farming emerged. Over the years New Denmark attracted many immigrants. In 1927 there were as many as 700 Danes in the area. New Denmark became the first major Danish settlement in Canada. It has to this day preserved an interest and a pride in its Danish heritage.

By the turn of the century the trickle of immigrants into Canada had become an ever-increasing flow. This was primarily due to the Canadian Pacific Railway. The CPR is closely connected

with the history of Canada. After surmounting obstacles of legendary proportions the CPR had completed the construction of the trans-continental railroad through Canada in 1885. The importance of this railroad can hardly be overstated. It linked together this vast country and played a key role in the development and settling of the Canadian West.

Among other remunerations the CPR was granted huge tracts of arable land along its lines (25 million acres, or an area about twice the size of Denmark.) In the following years numerous Danish settlers bought land from the CPR.

By the 1920's the CPR had established itself in Europe, and thus one of the largest transportation empires in the world had come to be. A network of CPR offices and agents sold tickets to their own Atlantic liners and their railways in Canada. Up to World Wor I, however, the direct immigration into Canada was never more than

5 % that of the United States. From 1868-1914, 255,000 Danes emigrated to the United States; only 12,000 Danes went directly to Canada during the same period. The statistics in this field are a moot point, though. The border between the United States and Canada was open, so the moment the immigrants had passed through Ellis Island, N.Y., or one of the Canadian ports of immigration, it was impossible to see whether they might have crossed the border to the other country, either right away or on a later occasion. As we shall see, some of the best-known Danish settlements in Canada were due to indirect immigration. A Canadian census from 1921 found 21,124 Danish-born citizens in Canada.

After World War I Danish emigration to Canada increased dramatically. The columns below indicate that from 1927 through 1929, Canada received more Danes than the United States:

Emigration from Denmark to Canada and the United States

Source: Danish Yearbook of Statistics.

Year	Canada	United States
1926	1,484	3,354
1927	3,835	2,962
1928	3,891	3,089
1929	2,982	2,748
1930	1,307	1,595

How is it that for three succesive years Canada was the prime target for Danish emigration to North America? One reason was the introduction of a quota system in 1921 to limit the number of immigrants admitted into the United States. Another reason was that the persistent sales drive carried out by the CPR (often as if it had governmental authority) really began to pay off. At this time the CPR had a sales office in Copenhagen (Nyhavn) and busy agents all over the country. Posters and pamphlets about the great opportunities in Canada, and on the prairies in particular, were distributed in astonishing numbers.

It is a puzzling fact that on the eve of the Great Depression and at a time when ominous tremors ran through the Canadian economy, Canada's appeal was greater than ever. The well-oiled transportation and sales system of the CPR continued to pump immigrants into western Canada when the economy of the country was already under a great strain. At this time it could no longer absorb the many new hands. In 1933, 20 % of the Canadian labor force was out of work, and many Danes who could afford to do so returned to Denmark.

If we look at the factors at work in favor of immigration to Canada, it is obvious that Canada caught the fancy of vast numbers of people in the bleak and dreary 1920s. Canada was a popular topic in Danish newspapers. Even though they were not allowed to openly advertize for emigration, there were indirect ways of doing so.

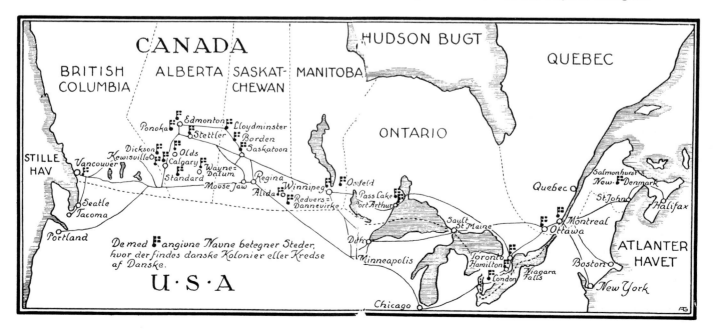

Danish clergymen from Canada visiting Denmark offered advice and wrote about the conditions in Canada for the Danish newspapers, and also addressed large audiences throughout the country. They reiterated again and again that the emigrant should go to a settlement in Canada with a Danish church. It is interesting to note that in the late 1920's there was a close co-operation between the CPR and the Danish clergy in western Canada.

On the whole, if we compare the Danish emigrant from before World War I with the emigrant of the 1920's, there is a distinct difference. The harsh social conditions that had "pushed" numerous Danes out of the country were no longer as prevalent. It is also clear that Canada and the CPR primarily wanted immigrants to settle the vast agricultural areas of western Canada. Throughout the 1920's it was emphasized that what was needed was agricultural laborers and in particular people who had money enough for a down payment on a farm. As the 1930's approached the importance of bringing along investment capital was stressed repeatedly, and it is a fact that in the 1920's, many Danish immigrants brought along not only their own two hands but also some capital to start with. Even though this was the case, it was always said that lots of hard work was a necessary and unfailing means of success. The Depression proved that notion wrong: now many failed despite their hard work.

Why Emigrate? Push and Pull in the 1920's

The decade of the 1920's certainly saw its share of social problems. In 1927 there were more than 100,000 (30 % of the work force) unemployed in Denmark. Many farmers who had invested during the war years when any product could be sold at a high price were caught by falling prices after the war and found themselves working very hard without any hope of improvement. The rumblings from the Weimar Republic in a state of dissolution also seemed to darken the hopes for a future in Denmark and throughout Europe.

Apart from "push" elements like these there were quite a number of "pull" factors which strongly affected the decision-making process in favor of emigration. There were successful emigrants visiting the old country as living examples of the North American success myth. It was often rumored that their passage was paid for by the CPR. There were numerous letters home written, for the most part by immigrants who had good

Regina, Saskatchewan.

news to report and would not mind the company of more countrymen to break the isolation and loneliness so often prevalent among immigrants. The most important and visible element, however, was the work done by the CPR and its agents.

The Emigration Pamphlet

The most readily-available source of information about Canada and the opportunities in that country during the 1920's were the thousands of free pamphlets distributed by the CPR sales office and its network of agents. Informational material was also distributed by the Canadian National Railways (CNR) which by then had an information office in Copenhagen. It did not matter whether the pamphlets came from the privately-owned CPR or the publicly-owned CNR – the message was the same: the stated purpose was not to persuade people to emigrate but if they had already made the decision, then the railways could be relied upon to furnish the best kind of information because of their close ties with the Canadian government.

All pamphlets that appeared throughout the 1920's offered a coast-to-coast review of the Canadian economy and geography with a clear emphasis on the areas where the Danes were wanted in particular (i.e. the prairie provinces of Manitoba, Saskatchewan, and Alberta). If we look at the CPR pamphlet from 1930 (a booklet of 110 pages, of which 70 are text), we find a wealth of information of both a direct and a subtle nature.

The 40 pages of photographs from all over Canada gave the impression of a very rich and fertile country. From the prairies there are only pictures of huge harvesting machines and bumper crops: no indication of what the landscape was really like. Immigrants whose image of Canada had been shaped by these pamphlets were in for a big surprise when they moved into an often treeless and boundless landscape. Not one of the many persuasive pictures showed that winter is a Canadian fact. On the contrary the Canadian winter is referred to as a "real blessing" (CPR, 1926). It is "healthy", makes the mortality rate one of the lowest in the world, and makes it possible "to buy food cheap in quantity because it can keep." In short these pamphlets, although claiming to contain only authorized and accurate information about Canada, are full of hidden persuasions. They insisted on the value and nobility of hard work, just as they warned that Canada was not for the weak and lazy. A statement taken from a speech by a Saskatchewan premier was often quoted: "Canada is a country full of milk and honey, but only for those who will milk the cows and keep the bees." At the end of the pamphlet was found a collection of letters from satisfied customers by then well-established in Canada.

The Danish Settlements in Canada

Before World War I and during the 1920s, most Danes went to places where other Danes had already settled, often to places where a Danish church had been established as a center and preserver of Danish language and culture. Danish clergymen were often very active in increasing the membership of their congregations.

Danish settlements can be found from the Anapolis Valley in Nova Scotia in the East to Vancouver Island in the West. Often a Dane settled, and then if he wanted neighbors, he would write back home to Denmark. In the case of Pass Lake, Ontario, the government set aside land specifically for Danish development. In 1926 there were 50 Danish settlers who homesteaded in that area. It was woodland that under certain conditions could be bought for 62.5 cents per acre.

In 1917 the Danish Church founded Dalum, a settlement near the coal mining town of Wayne, Alberta. The village hall is being built.

Some of the best-known Danish settlements in western Canada were founded by Danes who came from established Danish settlements in the United States in order to buy land. These settlements were quite numerous. There were too many to list them all here, but Standard, Alberta, is a good example.

In 1910 a group of Danish immigrants from Elk Horn, Iowa, were attracted by the extensive advertising of land made by the CPR. When the Elk Horn Danes responded, a 17,000-acre block of land was reserved for a Danish settlement. As was the case in many other settlements, a clergyman from the Danish Lutheran Church in the United States was among the very first settlers. The settlement became very successful and was often used as a showpiece in Denmark.

In 1926 there were about 1,000 Danes in the area around Standard. Its success attracted a lot of Danes directly from Denmark. Mr Anton M. Rasmussen of Standard was often pointed out as a prime example of Danish success in Canada. Apart from owning three farms, he managed others. He was a lumber merchant, a CPR agent, and was appointed to countless honorary jobs in his community. In 1928 he was instrumental in founding, and was elected president of the *Danish Immigration Aid Society of Canada*. He was also secretary of the Danish Folk High School in Calgary.

Dickson, Alberta, is another settlement founded by Danes coming up from the U.S. (Omaha, Nebraska, in 1902). Near Wayne, Alberta, Dalum was founded in 1918 under the auspices of *Dansk Folkesamfund* (The Danish Folk Society).

Dansk Folkesamfund had been founded in the United States by F.L. Grundtvig who was the son of N.F.S. Grundtvig, the inspiration behind the Danish Folk High School movement. Dansk Folkesamfund negotiated with the CPR, and a block of land was reserved primarily for Danish settlement. Dalum was the only settlement in the west with a Danish church belonging to the Grundtvigian branch of the Danish Lutheran Church.

The difference between the two branches – the *Grundtvigians* and the *Indre Mission* (Inner Mission) – so familiar in Denmark – had often led to agitated theological discussions in the new world. The dominant branch in Canada was the Indre Mission, based upon the ideas of Wilhelm Beck of Denmark, who favored an orthodox interpretation of Lutheran Christianity and strong church discipline, hence the nickname "Holy

Danish-Canadian farm ab. 1930.

Danes". In the United States and Canada they were in favor of cultural assimilation. This was in contrast to the Grundtvigians, or the so-called "Happy Danes", whose religion was more optimistic, and who, in cultural questions, were strongly in favor of preserving the Danish language and culture abroad.

Pastor Peter Rasmussen of Dalum was not only a very popular leader of the congregation that he served from 1920 to 1955, but he also won the respect of numerous other Danes in Canada. In 1921 he founded Dalum High School where, in agreement with the ideas of the Danish Folk High School, he taught a variety of basic subjects to adult students who often had nothing else to do during the winter. The clergyman in a large Danish settlement regularly served small groups of Danes in the vicinity. Thus Pastor Rasmussen also served Holden, Bingville and Huxley in the same part of Alberta.

In Saskatchewan and Manitoba there were a number of well-known Danish settlements. One in particular was frequently referred to in Danish newspapers, namely Dannevirke near Redvers and Alida, Saskatchewan. One Simon P. Hjortnes, who came up from the U.S. in 1901 and eventually settled near Alida, seems to have been the archetypal Danish pioneer. Legends of his toughness, successes and survival instincts have endured to this day. The Danish-Norwegian writer Aksel Sandemose based his novel *Ross Dane* (Nybyggerne i Alberta) largely on this historical figure of almost mythical proportions.

Further to the east in Manitoba, Ostenfeld was founded in 1926 by Pastor Niels Damskov, a

Danish immigrant chaplain in Winnipeg. He arranged with the Manitoba provincial government for a block land east of Winnipeg to be set aside for Danish settlers. Most of the Danes who went to Canada in the 1920s passed through Winnipeg, the "Gateway to the Canadian West". Most of them must have met Pastor Damskov who worked in co-operation with the government to help Danish immigrants on their way. He personally met all the immigrant trains arriving in Winnipeg, wearing his flat-visored officer's cap (see picture).

The Influx of Danes in the 1950s

Throughout the 1920s there was, as has been stated, an ever-increasing direct immigration of Danes into Canada. This influx came to a halt when, in the early 1930s, Canada stopped immigration except for close relatives. During the Great Depression many more Danes returned from than left for Canada. It is surprising, though, that the greatest and most concentrated influx of Danes occurred in the 1950s when Canada opened its doors to skilled labor and professionals.

From 1951 to 1958 no less than 22,000 Danes

The church in Redvers.

emigrated to Canada. In 1957 more than 7,143 Danes left the country: an all time high for Canada. This happened at a time when Denmark was struggling with a post-war recession and, consequently, a high unemployment rate. In contrast to earlier immigration, this new wave of Danes settled in major towns throughout Canada.

Dalum. Arrival.

Danish Culture in Canada Today

Before looking at the status of Danish culture or "Danishness" in present-day Canada, it is necessary to look at the typical Danish immigrant. From the very beginning of the official Canadian drive for immigration, Scandinavians seem to have been the most preferred immigrants after those from the British Isles. In 1921 the "White Star Dominion Line" advertized in Denmark that on board their emigrant liners, the Scandinavians and British would have their own dining-rooms. In Canada Danes always seem to have been met with great sympathy by the Canadian authorities and the Canadian people. In popular Canadian jokes there is no Danish stereotype, unlike what was often the case with other ethnic minorities like Swedes, Ukrainians, Poles, and Germans. There are a number of reasons for this.

In attempting a very cautious generalization, it can be said that the Danes who arrived in Canada from the late 19th century till present have been in many ways well-equipped. They hardly ever came completely empty-handed. They may not have spoken much English in the early days, but they had all received more education than the average immigrant from Europe. They were

Danish-Canadian farm ab. 1930.

not refugees that had been pushed or kicked out of their country for religious or political reasons, as was the case with some of the ethnic minorities that constitute the Canadian mosaic. On the whole the Danish immigrant seems to have been highly-motivated for a change of country and culture. The less-motivated Danes could always return to the old country, and many did, especially in the 1930s when socio-economic conditions in Canada were far worse than in Denmark. The

Dalum. First settlement.

same thing occurred in the 1960's when many Danes who had left for Canada in the 1950s returned to take part in the "roaring sixties" in Denmark. As a matter of fact the recent immigrants who stayed on became Canadian citizens as fast as possible and assimilated very quickly into the population at large. This process went on at a slower rate if the immigrant had begun the Canadian experience in one of the older Danish settlements. Even in the older settlements, however, a dilution of the Danishness started as early as the 1920s. For example, Danish as the language used in church was given up in Standard by 1929. In Dalum, Pastor Rasmussen preached in both Danish and English until his retirement in 1955.

The era in Canadian history when the Danish settlements in Canada existed as bastions of Danish culture is over. Most of the churches have lost their Danish character. Throughout Canada today there are only six Danish churches or congregations that receive support from *Dansk Kirke i Udlandet,* (The Danish Church Abroad). They are located in Toronto and Grimsby, Ontario; Edmonton, Calgary; and two in Vancouver, British Columbia.

There are, however, many Danish clubs and associations founded for various purposes. Some years ago Danish churches and clubs across Canada agreed to establish the "Federation of Danish Associations in Canada" in order to strengthen Danishness in Canada. Among the founders was Mr. Rolf Buschardt Christensen, an Ottawan, who is now the very resourceful president of the Association.

A Danish visitor to Canada cannot help being impressed with the loyalty to Denmark that is often found, even in second- and third-generation Danish-Canadians. This loyalty to their Danish heritage does not interfere with their overall loyalty to and pride in their new country. It indeed indicates the success of Canada's cultural policy which is based on the existence and vigor of many cultures. According to the 1981 census there are about 90,000 Canadians with roots in Denmark. There may not be a Danish street in Montreal or a Danish residential area in Toronto, but the Edmonton telephone directory (January 1985), for example, contains an unmistakable Danish presence in the 179 Jensens, 148 Nielsens, 142 Christensens, 59 Rasmussens, 39 Christiansens, and 9 Carlsens among its listings.

Dalum. Expansion.

Danes in Omaha, Nebraska, celebrating the 75th anniversary of the state in 1929.

The Rebild National Park.

A group of Danish immigrants in Chicago, led by the chemist Max Henius, founded The Danish-American Society in 1906. In 1910 the same group organized the purchase of an area of great scenic beauty in Jutland, Denmark _ the heathery hills of Rebild near Aalborg. This area was donated to the Danish state on condition that a festival be celebrated in the park every year on the Fourth of July. The first festival was held in 1912, and ever since thousands of people have gathered in the hills of Rebild to celebrate the American Independence Day. The Rebild Society, founded at the time of the purchase in 1910, still has many members both in Denmark and in the US.

A fascinating view is shown here: A section of wind turbine farms in Altamont Pass, Livermore, California. In front you see a NORDTANK A/S wind turbine.

Windmill on the Nebraska prairie, 1880.

The World's first Offshore Wind Farm. The Offshore Wind Farm was built by NORDTANK A/S for the Ebeltoft Energy Foundation and consists of 16 55/11 kW turbines. In addition, a 100 kW NORDTANK wind turbine is erected close to the control building which houses the computer terminal that monitors the wind turbines. The expected annual production of the wind farm is 2.8-3.0 millions kWh, which corresponds to 13 % of the electricity consumption of the Town of Ebeltoft.

Old Danish windmill rebuilt in Elk Horn, Iowa.

SAS ad inserted in Trade Magazines 1954.

SAS makes the dream come true